The Role of Science in the Criminal Justice System

There is increased interest in forensic science and a great deal of debate about the admissibility and reliability of not only new methods but also traditional scientific methods that have resulted in wrongful convictions. Many universities now offer programs in forensic science, either separately or as part of a criminal justice curriculum, in on-campus and online settings. This book offers an overview of forensic evidence, evidence collection, and analysis practices, and the uses of such evidence in casework. By doing so, it provides insight into the processes and procedures, who is considered an expert in a particular discipline, and how these factors impact the usage, reliability, and admissibility of evidence in the courts. Part I of the book outlines the concept of admissible evidence and the legal standards used by courts to determine if expert testimony is reliable enough for a jury to consider in determining guilt or innocence. Part II is about the "who" disciplines, describing the admissibility and reliability of a variety of pattern identification disciplines, including deoxyribonucleic acid (DNA), fingerprints, hair comparison, ballistics (toolmarks), handwriting, footwear, and digital forensics. Part III describes the admissibility and reliability issues in a variety of "how" disciplines, including fire and explosions, gunshot residue, blood pattern analysis, and medical examiner testimony. Part IV describes the uses of science by law enforcement and private companies outside the courtroom, including the advent of genetic genealogy as an investigative tool. The final part discusses the future of forensic science, including the use of artificial intelligence (AI) and potential changes in law, regulatory, and educational requirements.

The Role of Science in the Criminal Justice System

Donald E. Shelton

CRC Press
Taylor & Francis Group
Boca Raton London

CRC Press is an imprint of the
Taylor & Francis Group, an **informa** business

Designed cover image: Shutterstock

First edition published 2026
by CRC Press
2385 NW Executive Center Drive, Suite 320, Boca Raton FL 33431

and by CRC Press
4 Park Square, Milton Park, Abingdon, Oxon, OX14 4RN

CRC Press is an imprint of Taylor & Francis Group, LLC

ISBN: 978-1-041-13631-6 (hbk)
ISBN: 978-1-041-13632-3 (pbk)
ISBN: 978-1-041-13636-1 (ebk)

DOI: 10.4324/9781041136361

Typeset in Palatino
by Apex CoVantage, LLC

CONTENTS

PART II The Reliability of Pattern Identifications

Part IV The Use of Forensic Science out of Court

Part V The Future of Forensic Science Evidence

ABOUT THE AUTHOR

Hon. Donald E. Shelton (ret.) was a circuit judge in Ann Arbor, Michigan, for almost 25 years. During his time on the bench, he served as Chief Judge of the Circuit, Juvenile, and Probate Courts. The Michigan Constitution requires that judges leave the bench at age 70. After retiring from the bench, he was a professor at the University of Michigan Dearborn and the director of the Criminology and Criminal Justice Program and the director of the university's Justice Reform Project. Born in Jackson, Michigan, Judge Shelton earned his undergraduate degree from Western Michigan University, his Juris Doctor degree from the University of Michigan Law School, his master's degree in Criminology and Criminal Justice from Eastern Michigan University, and his Ph.D. in Judicial Studies from the University of Nevada Reno. Dr. Shelton is a prolific author, particularly in the field of forensic science evidence. His doctoral dissertation was *Criminal Adjudication: The Challenges of Forensic Science Evidence in the Early 21st Century*, and his earlier books include *Forensic Science in Court: Challenges in the 21st Century* and *Forensic Science Evidence: Can the Law Keep Up with Science?*. He has published many articles and research papers and was one of the earliest published researchers into the so-called CSI Effect and the expectation of jurors for scientific evidence. Judge Shelton is a fellow in the American Academy of Forensic Sciences and the past chair of the AAFS Jurisprudence Section. He continues to teach forensic science and criminal justice and recently served as a member and committee chair of the Michigan Governor's Forensic Science Task Force.

FIGURES

INTRODUCTION

The use of science to solve crimes goes back to ancient times when an autopsy was used to determine the cause of a death. It flourished in the 19th century when police developed the use of fingerprints and ballistics. The invention of the dual microscope in the early 1900s led police to more effective fingerprint and ballistic analysis and to its use in several other pattern identification techniques. During that same time, the idea of trace evidence emerged when Edmond Locard pioneered the "exchange principle" concept that everything and everyone that enters a crime scene leaves some piece of evidence behind.

The 21st century saw scientific breakthroughs, especially in information technology and the development of the internet. Police and prosecutors were quick to use those developments in criminal cases. The most significant development in criminal justice in the last 200 years came with the discovery of deoxyribonucleic acid (DNA). Unlike most traditional forensic sciences, DNA was not developed in a police laboratory or even for use in criminal cases. However, the subsequent idea of DNA profiling to identify individuals from the DNA patterns in every cell of their body proved to be the most accurate form of human identification the justice system had ever seen.

DNA also had another very important impact on the criminal justice system. While it has the uncanny ability to identify perpetrators of crime, it has the equal ability to exonerate innocent suspects. That led to the discovery that many innocent people had been wrongfully convicted. The forensic science system was rocked when it turned out that a significant number of wrongful convictions had been based on traditional forensic science evidence. That led to a reexamination of the scientific basis of many forms of forensic science that had been routinely admitted by judges in criminal cases. This book reviews how the criminal justice system has responded, or not, to those reexaminations.

Part I is a general description of how courts determine if forensic science evidence is allowed in criminal prosecutions. Chapter 1 describes the concept of admissibility and the role of the judge as the "gatekeeper" of what evidence the jury is allowed to see. Chapter 2 is a discussion of the principles and rules that have developed for judges to make those admissibility decisions. It reviews the important cases, including the *Frye* and

Daubert cases, that provide the criteria to be used by judges, as well as the rules of evidence that must be followed. Chapter 3 discusses "bad science" and reviews the findings of the National Academy of Sciences (NAS) Report about the questionable state of many forensic science techniques. Chapter 4 discusses the basic dissonance between the law and science and suggests reasons why the judicial system resists change, including changes in science.

Part II specifically describes reliability issues with several forms of pattern identification used by law enforcement. Chapter 5 is a discussion of how pattern identification has been used to try to associate a particular piece of trace evidence with a specific person and the problem with declaring a "match" or using similar terms that are unwarranted by the science. In succeeding Chapters 6–12, we examine DNA, hair comparison, fingerprints, ballistics, handwriting, digital forensics, and footwear comparison.

Part III is about forensic science evidence that is used to determine how a particular event happened. Chapters 13–15 look at fire and explosions, bloodstains and patterns, and gunshot residue. Chapter 16 discusses the history and role of medical examiners, or coroners, in criminal proceedings and discusses the debate over medical examiner testimony as to the manner of death, rather than just the cause of death.

While the focus has been on the admissibility of forensic science evidence at a criminal trial, some forms of scientific evidence may be used for non-criminal purposes or just as an investigative tool that might lead to admissible evidence in a criminal case. Part IV is a description of a few of those tools. Chapter 17 describes tools that are used for non-criminal purposes, including forensic odontology to identify human remains, death certificates for public health programs, and polygraphs for employment and other purposes. Chapter 18 describes criminal investigation tools that may lead to admissible evidence, including pattern identifications, polygraphs, and the growing fields of facial recognition and genetic genealogy.

Finally, Part V looks at some ideas about the future of forensic science evidence. Chapter 19 discusses the role artificial intelligence (AI) tools may play in the development or refining of forensic science techniques. It also reviews some of the advantages and challenges posed by AI in criminal justice. Chapter 20 discusses some pathways to improve the forensic science system and the problems presented by our adversarial justice system. There is a review of the potential changes in the education of lawyers and judges and a discussion of the likelihood of legislative changes, as well as the use of forensic science commissions or other oversight boards to further investigate the reliability and use of forensic science evidence.

Part I

The Use of Forensic Science in the Courtroom

1

The Concept of Admissibility

The word "forensic" comes from the Latin word "forensic," which means "forum" or "public." The modern understanding is that "forensic" means the public forum of the legal system. As the adjective in "forensic science," it came to mean science that is related to legal investigations and court proceedings. It is not pure or basic science, which is based on developing theories to explain natural phenomena. Forensic science is applied rather than pure science. It is the application of scientific theories and methodology to practical issues, particularly legal issues or disputes.

1.1 JUDGES AND JURIES

The legal process in the United States is based on accusation, investigation, and resolution. Forensic science can be used to apply scientific principles or theories at any of those stages. Ultimately the forum for resolution of a legal issue is a trial, in which a judge presides as the source of law and a jury of citizens decides the facts – what happened. To determine those facts, jurors see and hear evidence from witnesses who say under oath what they observed or heard. It is for the jury to decide whether that testimony proves, either directly or circumstantially, that the defendant committed the crime with which he is charged. The legal standard is that the jury must be convinced beyond a reasonable doubt of those facts before a defendant may be found guilty.

Normally witnesses give what is called "lay" testimony. They describe only what they saw or heard and not their conclusions or opinions about those observations. Sometimes there are issues that ordinary jurors do not have the knowledge or experience to understand. In those situations, an

DOI: 10.4324/9781041136361-2

expert's special knowledge may help the jury understand the importance of the factual evidence it hears. Such an expert witness can give opinion testimony when those opinions would assist the jury in reaching that ultimate issue. Testimony from scientific experts is the classic form of such expert testimony. As applied to our system, forensic science evidence is the observation and opinion of a trained person that is designed to aid the jury in understanding the meaning or conclusions that are suggested by the factual evidence. The testimony may relate to whether there is scientific evidence that the alleged act even occurred, such as biological or psychological evidence about a sexual assault. Identification of the defendant as the person who committed an act is the subject of such areas as DNA, fingerprints, handwriting analysis, and hair analysis. The question of how an event occurred is often addressed in such areas as medical examinations, ballistics, fire, explosion and arson testimony, and bloodstain pattern analysis.

1.2 THE CONCEPT OF ADMISSIBILITY

So what kinds of evidence should the jury consider in deciding whether the defendant is guilty beyond a reasonable doubt? The basic legal term is "relevance." Does the evidence have "probative value"? In other words, does this evidence tend to prove or disprove that the defendant committed the crime being charged? The law has developed rules about what evidence a jury should consider. The rules in federal court include Federal Rules 402 and 403.

RULE 402 GENERAL ADMISSIBILITY OF RELEVANT EVIDENCE

Relevant evidence is admissible unless any of the following provides otherwise:

- The U.S. Constitution
- A federal statute
- These rules
- Other rules prescribed by the Supreme Court

Irrelevant evidence is not admissible.

So, admissibility simply means whether the jury should hear and consider the evidence. Generally, evidence that tends to prove or disprove guilt or innocence should be heard. Think about some evidence that may not be relevant:

- Testimony from an astrology person about the position of the moon and stars on the date of the crime
- Testimony that most crimes are committed by men rather than women
- Testimony that the defendant has the reputation of being an immoral person
- Testimony that the defendant is of a particular religion or is an atheist

But there are exceptions. Sometimes, while some evidence may have a tendency to prove guilt or innocence, it still may not be appropriate for a jury to hear or consider. It may be too prejudicial, meaning that it is more an appeal to the jurors' emotions than proof of an element of the crime. For example, should all 50 gruesome pictures taken at the autopsy of an alleged murder victim be considered just to prove that the person is dead? Should evidence of a confession be heard by the jury if the defendant was beaten into making the confession? Should evidence from a search of the defendant's home be heard by the jury if the police illegally broke into the home?

RULE 403 EXCLUDING RELEVANT EVIDENCE FOR PREJUDICE, CONFUSION, WASTE OF TIME, OR OTHER REASONS

The court may exclude relevant evidence if its probative value is substantially outweighed by a danger of one or more of the following: unfair prejudice, confusing the issues, misleading the jury, undue delay, wasting time, or needlessly presenting cumulative evidence.

1.3 THE JUDGE AS "GATEKEEPER"

An important part of this chapter is an understanding that the judge must decide what evidence the jury will hear or see. The judge has the responsibility to determine what evidence is admissible and what is not. White (2015).

Admissibility of evidence is a legal issue, and the judge decides all legal, as opposed to factual, issues in a trial. The jury decides the facts, while the judge decides the law. This basic concept is that the judge is the "gatekeeper" of all evidence in the sense that he or she decides what evidence comes into a jury trial and what evidence does not. Federal Rule 104 simply states that the judge "must decide any preliminary question about whether a witness is qualified, a privilege exists, or evidence is admissible." Fed. R. Evid. 104.

The gatekeeping responsibility of judges applies to all evidence, and this includes testimony from expert witnesses. The basic rule concerning expert witnesses is Federal Rule 702.

RULE 702 TESTIMONY BY EXPERT WITNESSES

A witness who is qualified as an expert by knowledge, skill, experience, training, or education may testify in the form of an opinion or otherwise if the proponent demonstrates to the court that it is more likely than not that

(a) the expert's scientific, technical, or other specialized knowledge will help the trier of fact to understand the evidence or to determine a fact in issue;
(b) the testimony is based on sufficient facts or data;
(c) the testimony is the product of reliable principles and methods;
(d) the expert's opinion reflects a reliable application of the principles and methods to the facts of the case.

Is the expert qualified? Will the testimony help the jury? Does it have a basis in fact? Is it reliable? Has the witness properly applied his or her expertise to this case? This understanding of the gatekeeping role of the judge in deciding whether to admit evidence is crucial to an understanding of how forensic science can and cannot be used in the legal system (Figure 1.1).

Figure 1.1 Admissible Evidence.

Source: Nick Youngson, Pix4free.org

REFERENCES

Fed. R. Evid. 104
Fed. R. Evid. 402
Fed. R. Evid. 403
Fed. R. Evid. 702
White, P., *Federal Rules of Evidence: Role of Judges in the Evidentiary Process*, National Judicial College (2015) https://www.judges.org/news-and-info/judicial-news-judicial-edge-federal-rules-of-evidence/

READINGS

Findley, K., *Judicial Gatekeeping of Suspect Evidence: Due Process and Evidentiary Rules in the Age of Innocence*, 47 Ga. Law Rev. (2012–2013) https://georgialawreview.org/wp-content/uploads/2025/01/Keith-A.-Findley-Judicial-Gatekeeping-of-Suspect-Evidence-Due-Process-and-Evidentiary-Rules-47-Georgia-Law-Review-2013.pdf

Grimm, P., *Challenges Facing Judges Regarding Expert Evidence in Criminal Cases,* 86 Fordham Law Rev. (2017–2018) https://fordhamlawreview.org/issues/challenges-facing-judges-regarding-expert-evidence-in-criminal-cases/

Justia, *Admissibility of Evidence in Criminal Law Cases* https://www.justia.com/criminal/procedure/admissibility-evidence/

Williams, S., *Evidence: The Concept of 'Admissibility',* https://www.findlaw.com/criminal/criminal-procedure/evidence-the-concept-of-admissibility.html

2

Judicial Rules for Admissibility of Forensic Science Evidence

As discussed in Chapter 1, the judge must decide what evidence the jury will hear. How does that work when the proposed evidence comes from an expert, especially when the expert testimony is scientifically based? Should it be just a matter of whether the witness has the qualifications, the degrees, or the certifications, in his or her field? Or should the judge somehow make sure that the testimony is about a real or reliable science? If so, how would a judge know whether the science is real or "junk"? Until the early 20th century, these questions basically went unanswered. And then in 1923, an opinion in a Court of Appeals case in Washington, D.C., would become the rule for the admissibility of forensic science testimony for the next 70+ years. The case was *Frye v. United States*, and the rule would become known as the "*Frye* test."

2.1 FRYE V. UNITED STATES

In *Frye v. United States*, 54 App. D.C. 46, 293 F. 1013 (1923), the defendant in a murder trial claimed he was innocent and wanted his expert witness to testify that the defendant had passed an early version of a "lie detector test." The trial judge refused to admit the evidence and said that only the jury could decide if the defendant was telling the truth or not. After his conviction Frye appealed to the District of Columbia Court of Appeals. The appeals court upheld the conviction and the judge's decision

DOI: 10.4324/9781041136361-3

to exclude the expert's testimony. The language of the short opinion would become the standard for judges to determine the admissibility of new or novel forensic science evidence. The court said:

> [W]hile courts will go a long way in admitting expert testimony deduced from a well-recognized scientific principle or discovery, the thing from which the deduction is made must be sufficiently established to have gained general acceptance in the particular field in which it belongs.
>
> Frye v. U.S. at p. 1014.

The lie detector did not meet that test.

> We think the systolic blood pressure deception test has not yet gained such standing and scientific recognition among physiological and psychological authorities as would justify the courts in admitting expert testimony deduced from the discovery, development, and experiments thus far made.
>
> Frye v. U.S. at p. 1014.

This principle has become known as the *Frye* or "general acceptance" test. That test says that evidence based on a new scientific technique or instrument will only be admitted if it has been established that specialists in the field where the technique belongs have generally accepted the technique as reliable based on sound scientific principles. General acceptance is in effect the "consensus" test, where a scientific principle is not acceptable in the court system until most of the scientists in that field have accepted it. Proof of the general acceptance of the scientific technique is the sole condition for the admission of scientific testimony under *Frye*. Although the *Frye* rule was technically applicable only in the District of Columbia, the test spread throughout the United States as other judges read it and adopted it as a rule in their jurisdictions. The general acceptance test became the governing law in almost all federal courts and almost all of the states.

2.2 JAMES FRYE AND THE LIE DETECTOR

On November 28, 1920, a well-known doctor in Washington, D.C., Dr. R. W. Brown, was shot and killed in his home office. A witness in the house who heard the shots described the shooter as a light-brown-skinned man, 24–25 years old, weighing 135 pounds. There were four gunshots, and a .45-caliber revolver was left on the floor. A year later, the police arrested James A. Frye for a different crime, and he confessed to the killing of Dr. Brown but claimed it was in self-defense following an argument over the doctor's fee. He was charged with first-degree premeditated murder. Frye recanted his confession and said it was just part of a deal with the police interrogator to share some reward money.

Frye's appointed attorneys contacted a psychologist, Dr. William Marston, who had recently invented a machine called a "Systolic Blood Pressure Deception Test," a sphygmomanometer, that he said could detect if a person was lying or telling the truth – the first "lie detector." Dr. Marston administered the test to Frye and said that he was telling the truth and had nothing to do with the murder (Figure 2.1). At the trial, however, the judge would not admit the results of the lie detector test or allow Marston to testify as an expert. The judge stated that lie detection was not "a matter of common knowledge" and that only the jury could decide if a witness was telling the truth. Unusually the argument over the

Figure 2.1 Dr. William Marston Checks James Frye's Pulse and Blood Pressure: A Simulation of the Systolic Blood Pressure Deception Test.

Source: Getty images

admissibility took place while the jury was present. The jury found Frye guilty of second-degree murder, and he was sentenced to life in prison. Frye appealed his conviction and the judge's decision to exclude the lie detector results to the Court of Appeals for the District of Columbia.

2.3 PROS AND CONS OF THE FRYE GENERAL ACCEPTANCE TEST

In effect, the *Frye* test delegates the admissibility decision to the scientific community. The person offering the testimony must show that most specialists within the relevant scientific discipline accept the theory. The *Frye* test effectively assigns the admissibility decision to those expert specialists. This is based on the concern that judges are not scientists and are incapable of judging whether a new scientific technique is valid or reliable. That scientific decision should be left to scientists and not to lawyers. Another justification is that if a witness is allowed to testify as an expert, a jury may be overly impressed with credentials and may just assume that his testimony is about good reliable science. The advocates of the *Frye* test believe that most lay jurors are incapable of weighing scientific testimony and will overestimate the probative value of the expert testimony.

Critics of the *Frye* rule do not accept these justifications. First, they believe that it abdicates the judicial function of the court to decide whether any evidence should be admitted. It is a judicial gatekeeping responsibility to decide whether to admit evidence during a trial, and they should not pass that responsibility to someone outside the legal system. Admittedly, judges are not trained in any particular science, but that does not mean that they should not make the legal decision entrusted to them. Judges are not expected to be experts in the fields where they are called upon to make decisions. The adversary process means that the lawyers will present evidence and arguments to educate and advise the judge so that he or she can make an informed judgment. Certainly, judges will defer to the expertise of scientists and should consider the consensus of scientists about a particular technique. But *Frye* goes beyond and has the effect of delegating the decision to scientists.

Perhaps the biggest criticism of the general acceptance test is that it ignores the speed at which science advances, particularly in the last century. The *Frye* test means that there will be a significant delay between the proven validity of a scientific theory and the admission of that proven science in court. It may take years before a valid scientific advancement is known to, much less accepted by, most of the scientists in a particular field. Publication of new studies and their results may take years to get actually published and distributed to the scientific community in professional journals. During that delay, even if a judge is convinced that the scientific theory is valid, the *Frye* rule does not allow the jury to hear about it when deciding guilt or innocence.

2.4 THE DAUBERT TRILOGY

Seventy years after the *Frye* case, the U.S. Supreme Court finally decided how judges should evaluate the admissibility of forensic science evidence. The justices rejected the *Frye* analysis. In Daubert v. Merrell Dow Pharmaceuticals, Inc., 509 U.S. 579 (1993), the Supreme Court said that the recently enacted Federal Rules of Evidence superseded any ruling in *Frye*. Federal Rule 702 at that time read:

> If scientific, technical, or other specialized knowledge will assist the trier of fact to understand the evidence or to determine a fact in issue, a witness qualified as an expert by knowledge, skill, experience, training, or education, may testify thereto in the form of an opinion or otherwise.
>
> Fed. R. Evid. 702

The Supreme Court stated:

> Nothing in the text of this Rule establishes "general acceptance" as an absolute prerequisite to admissibility. Nor does respondent present any clear indication that Rule 702 or the Rules as a whole were intended to incorporate a "general acceptance" standard. The drafting history makes no mention of *Frye*, and a rigid "general acceptance" requirement would be at odds with the "liberal thrust" of the Federal Rules and their "general approach of relaxing the traditional barriers to 'opinion' testimony."
>
> Daubert v. Merrell Dow (1993) at p. 588

Instead, the Court emphasized that the judge is always the "gatekeeper" of admissible evidence, and that the gatekeeper role applied to forensic science evidence as well. To fulfill that duty, the judge must make "a preliminary assessment of whether the reasoning or methodology underlying the testimony is scientifically valid, and of whether that reasoning or methodology properly can be applied to the facts in issue." (Daubert v. Merrell Dow (1993) at p. 580). The Court identified several factors that should be considered. Those factors are now what are considered the *Daubert* test for admissibility of forensic science evidence.

THE DAUBERT TEST

1. Whether the theory or technique can be and has been tested
2. The known or potential rate of error
3. The existence and maintenance of standards controlling the technique's operation
4. Publication (or lack thereof) in a peer-reviewed journal
5. General acceptance in the relevant scientific community

The Court emphasized that the test for reliability is "flexible" and that none of the factors by itself is determinative one way or the other.

2.5 THE JOINER AND KUMHO CASES

After the *Daubert* case, some important questions remained. In *General Electric Co. v. Joiner*, 522 U.S. 136 (1997), the Court clarified that the judge must find not only that the expert's theory or technique is reliable but also that the expert has reliably applied it to the facts of the particular case. The Court also said that once a trial judge has made a ruling on admissibility it will only be overturned if the judge abused his or her discretion in making the decision.

The third case in the *Daubert* trilogy is an important one. After the ruling in *Daubert*, some attorneys and judges thought that the *Daubert* test only applied to "scientific" evidence and that experts who offered "technical" testimony were not covered by the ruling. In *Kumho Tire Co., Ltd. v. Carmichael*, 526 U.S. 137 (1999), a van crash resulted in the death of one passenger and the injury of others. A tire manufactured by the Kumho company had blown out, and the van had overturned. The plaintiffs sued Kumho, claiming that the tire had been defectively manufactured. They presented the testimony of an engineer, Dennis Carlson, who inspected the tire and stated that a defect had caused the tread to separate, resulting in the blowout. The trial judge applied the *Daubert* factors and found that the methodology used by Carlson was not reliable and excluded the testimony. When the case got to the Supreme Court, Carmichael contended that the *Daubert* test should apply only to "scientific" evidence and not to the "technical" engineering testimony in the case. The Supreme Court disagreed. Again referring to the language of Federal Rule 702, the Court stated:

> This language makes no relevant distinction between "scientific" knowledge and "technical" or "other specialized" knowledge. It makes clear that any such knowledge might become the subject of expert testimony.
>
> . . .
>
> We conclude that *Daubert's* general principles apply to the expert matters described in Rule 702. Kumho Tire Co., Ltd. V. Carmichael, at pp. 147, 149

The importance of the *Kumho* case is that the *Daubert* test applies to all expert testimony.

2.6 FEDERAL RULE OF EVIDENCE 702

After the *Daubert* ruling in 1993, Congress amended Federal Rule of Evidence (FRE) 702 to incorporate the *Daubert* ruling. More recently in 2023, the Congress again amended the rule to correspond to and emphasize the obligation of the judge to be the gatekeeper of all expert testimony, including forensic science evidence. The newly amended rule makes it clear that the judge should hold a hearing to determine whether the evidence is reliable and has been reliably applied to the particular case. It also clarifies that the burden of proving its reliability is on the proponent, the person who wants to introduce the evidence, and that the proof must show that it is "more likely than not" both reliable and reliably applied.

RULE 702 TESTIMONY BY EXPERT WITNESSES

A witness who is qualified as an expert by knowledge, skill, experience, training, or education may testify in the form of an opinion or otherwise if the proponent demonstrates to the court that it is more likely than not that

(a) the expert's scientific, technical, or other specialized knowledge will help the trier of fact to understand the evidence or to determine a fact in issue;
(b) the testimony is based on sufficient facts or data;
(c) the testimony is the product of reliable principles and methods;
(d) the expert's opinion reflects a reliable application of the principles and methods to the facts of the case.

2.7 MORNING SICKNESS, BIRTH DEFECTS, AND THE SUPREME COURT

When Joyce Daubert became pregnant, she started to experience what was commonly called "morning sickness" – nausea and vomiting after waking up. Her doctor prescribed a drug called Bendectin to help with the nausea (Figure 2.2). Joyce took it three times during her first trimester but did not think it was very effective. On July 26, 1973, two weeks after her due date, she gave birth to a baby boy they named Jason. But Jason only had two fingers on his right hand, and his right arm was rigid at an odd angle. X-rays showed that Jason was missing a bone in his forearm, missing three fingers on his right hand, and had a hernia, an undescended testicle, and a deformed big toe (Figure 2.3).

Later, the Daubert family filed a lawsuit against Merrell Dow Pharmaceuticals, the company that made Bendectin, claiming that the drug had caused Jason's birth defects. Merrell Dow denied the claim and presented an affidavit from Steven H. Lamm, a physician and epidemiologist, who stated that he had reviewed all the published literature on Bendectin and birth defects and that no study had found Bendectin to be capable of causing birth defects. The company asked the judge to throw out the case. In response, however, the Dauberts presented the affidavits of eight experts who had concluded that Bendectin can cause birth defects. Their conclusions were based upon animal studies that found a link between Bendectin and malformations, studies of the chemical structure of Bendectin that was similar to other substances known to cause birth defects, and the "reanalysis" of previously published human studies. The trial judge applied the *Frye* rule and held the expert opinions based on animal studies rather than human studies were not "generally accepted" in the scientific community. He summarily dismissed the plaintiff's case. The Ninth Circuit Court of Appeals affirmed his decision and the Dauberts appealed to the U.S. Supreme Court.

The Supreme Court said that the *Frye* rule was not the proper test to be used to screen forensic science evidence and that the Federal Rules of Evidence (FRE) adopted by Congress did not include the *Frye* doctrine. Instead, the Court held that a trial judge, who is the "gatekeeper" of all evidence, should evaluate the reliability of the offered evidence based on five factors – whether the scientific theory had been tested; its error rate; whether there were established standards in the field; whether it had been published in peer-reviewed journals; and whether it was (like *Frye*)

Figure 2.2 Bendectin Advertisement 1966.

Figure 2.3 Jason Daubert 2020.

Source: Bendectin image – University of Wisconsin Library, https://digital.library.wisc.edu/1711.dl/KC2P7UTVPGN5D8K; Jason Daubert image from https://undark.org/2020/02/17/daubert-standard-joyce-jason/

generally accepted. They reversed the dismissal of the case. The ruling of the Supreme Court was the first major change in forensic science admissibility in 70 years.

But the Dauberts never did get their day in court. Rather than sending the case back to the trial court, the Ninth Circuit appeals judges reviewed the case again, supposedly applying the factors set out by the

Supreme Court. The appeals court said that the Daubert expert witnesses' conclusions were not reliable under those standards and again dismissed the case. Daubert v. Merrell Dow Pharmaceuticals, Inc., 43 F.3d 1311 (9th Cir. 1995) on remand. The Supreme Court refused to review the case again and Jason Daubert never got to have his case heard by a jury.

2.8 FEDERAL AND STATE COURTS – FEDERALISM AT WORK

So is *Frye* dead? Not so fast. In our system of federalism under the U.S. Constitution, power is shared between the States and the federal government. When it comes to the court system this means that the federal courts can only decide cases involving federal law and that all other cases are within the jurisdiction of the States. This means that almost all criminal cases are decided in State courts and not federal courts, although there may be some overlap. So the test for the admissibility of forensic science evidence in each State matters, especially in criminal cases. Each State has its own rules of evidence, and no State is obligated to follow the federal rules. On the other hand, a State may choose to follow the lead of the federal rules and may choose to adopt the ruling of a federal case, like *Daubert*, or not.

Many States have chosen to adopt the *Daubert* test and enact State rules of evidence that are similar to the federal rules, including FRE 702. The status of *Daubert* and similar rules of evidence as of 2025 is on the following page. Each State has fashioned its own version of the admissibility rules. *Daubert* is the dominant standard, but there are variations. And it gets just a little more complicated. Just because a State court has adopted the standards from the *Daubert* case does not mean that they adopt or agree with the interpretations of that standard in other federal cases. Therefore, even a State that has adopted the standards from the *Daubert* case may choose not to adopt the holding of the *Kumho* case that *Daubert* applies to all experts. For example, some States have chosen not to apply the *Daubert* standards to expert testimony from psychological or other social science witnesses (Figure 2.4).

State	Status of Daubert/Frye	Authority
Alabama	*Daubert* and *Frye* by case type	Evidence Rule 702
Alaska	*Daubert*	Evidence Rule 702
Arizona	*Daubert*	Evidence Rule 702
Arkansas	*Daubert*	Evidence Rule 702
Califiornia	*Frye/Kelly*	Cal. Evidence Code 702
Colorado	*Daubert/Shreck*	Evidence Rule 702
Connecticut	*Daubert/Porter*	Code of Evidence 7-2
Dist. of Columbia	*Daubert*	*Motorola v. Murray*
Delaware	*Daubert*	Uniform Rule of Evidence 702
Florida	*Daubert*	*In re Amendments to the Fla. Evid. Code*
Georgia	*Daubert*	Ga. Code of Evidence §24-7-702
Hawaii	modified *Daubert*	Hawaii Rev. Stat. Ann. 702
Idaho	modified *Daubert*	Evidence Rule 702
Illinois	*Frye* new or novel only	Evidence Rule 702
Indiana	modified *Daubert*	Evidence Rule 702
Iowa	modified *Daubert*	Evidence Rule 5.702
Kansas	*Daubert*	Kan. Stat. Ann 60-45(b)
Kentucky	*Daubert*	Evidence Rule 702
Louisiana	*Daubert*	Code of Evidence 702
Maine	Neither - reliability only	Evidence Rule 702
Maryland	*Daubert*	Evidence Rule 5-702
Massachusetts	*Daubert*	Evidence Rule 702
Michigan	*Daubert*	Evidence Rule 702
Minnesota	*Frye/Mack*	Evidence Rule 702
Mississippi	*Daubert*	Evidence Rule 702
Missouri	*Daubert*	Mo. Rev. Stat. §490.065
Montana	*Daubert*	Evidence Rule 702
Nebraska	*Daubert*	Neb. Rev. Stat.27-702
Nevada	revised *Daubert*	Nev, Rev. Stat. 50.275
New Hampshire	*Daubert*	Evidence Rule 702
New Jersey	*Daubert* and *Frye* by case type	Evidence Rule 702
New Mexico	*Daubert/Alberico*	Evidence Rule 702
New York	*Frye*	NY CPLR §R4515 (2016)
North Carolina	*Daubert*	Evidence Rule 702
North Dakota	Neither	*State v, Hernandez* 707 N.W.2d 449
Ohio	*Daubert*	Evidence Rule 702
State	**Status of Daubert/Frye**	**Authority**
Oklahoma	*Daubert*	Okla. Stat. §12-2702
Oregon	*Daubert/Brown*	ORS 40.410 702
Pennsylania	*Frye*	Evidence Rule 702
Rhode Island	*Daubert*	Evidence Rule 702
South Carolina	Neither	*State v, Jones*, 817 S.E.2d 268
South Dakota	*Daubert*	S. Dak. Cod. Laws 19-19-702
Tennessee	modified *Daubert*	Evidence Rule 702
Texas	modified *Daubert*	Evidence Rule 702
Utah	*Frye*	Evidence Rule 702
Vermont	*Daubert*	Evidence Rule 702
Virginia	modified *Daubert*	Evidence Rule 702
Washington	*Frye*	Evidence Rule 702
West Virginia	modified *Daubert*	*Wilt v. Buracker*, 443 S.E.2d 196
Wisconsin	*Daubert*	Wis. Rev. Stat. §907.02
Wyoming	*Daubert*	Evidence Rule 702

Figure 2.4 Funk, Status of Daubert in the States (2025).

CASE STUDY Frye v. United States, 54 App. D. C. 46, 293 F. 1013 (1923)

The decision of the court in Frye v. United States, 54 App. D. C. 46, 293 F. 1013 (1923):

Appellant, the defendant below, was convicted of the crime of murder in the second degree and from the judgment prosecutes this appeal.

A single assignment of error is presented for our consideration. During the trial, counsel for the defendant offered an expert witness to testify to the result of a deception test made upon the defendant. The test is described as the systolic blood pressure deception test. It is asserted that blood pressure is influenced by change in the emotions of the witness and that the systolic blood pressure rises are brought about by nervous impulses sent to the sympathetic branch of the autonomic nervous system. Scientific experiments, it is claimed, have demonstrated that fear, rage, and pain always produce a rise of systolic blood pressure and that conscious deception or falsehood, concealment of facts, or guilt of crime, accompanied by fear of detection when the person is under examination, raises the systolic blood pressure in a curve, which corresponds exactly to the struggle going on in the subject's mind between fear and attempted control of that fear, as the examination touches the vital points in respect of which he is attempting to deceive the examiner.

In other words, the theory seems to be that truth is spontaneous and comes without conscious effort, while the utterance of a falsehood requires a conscious effort, which is reflected in the blood pressure. The rise thus produced is easily detected and distinguished from the rise produced by mere fear of the examination itself. In the former instance, the pressure rises higher than in the latter and is more pronounced as the examination proceeds, while in the latter case, if the subject is telling the truth, the pressure registers highest at the beginning of the examination, and gradually diminishes as the examination proceeds.

Prior to the trial, defendant was subjected to this deception test, and counsel offered the scientist who conducted the test as an expert to testify to the results obtained. The offer was objected to by counsel for the government, and the court sustained the objection. Counsel for the defendant then offered to have the proffered witness conduct a test in the presence of the jury. This also was denied.

Counsel for defendant, in their able presentation of the novel question involved, correctly state in their brief that no cases directly in point have been found. The broad ground, however, upon which they plant their case, is succinctly stated in their brief as follows:

> The rule is that the opinions of experts or skilled witnesses are admissible in evidence in those cases in which the matter of inquiry is such that inexperienced persons are unlikely to prove capable of forming a correct judgment upon it, for the reason that the subject-matter so far partakes of a science, art, or trade as to require a previous habit or experience or study in it, in order to acquire a knowledge of it. When the question involved does not lie within the range of common experience or common knowledge, but requires special experience or special knowledge, then the opinions of witnesses skilled in that particular science, art, or trade to which the question relates are admissible in evidence.

Numerous cases are cited in support of this rule. Just when a scientific principle or discovery crosses the line between the experimental and demonstrable stages is difficult to define. Somewhere in this twilight zone the evidential force of the principle must be recognized, and while courts will go a long way in admitting expert testimony deduced from a well-recognized scientific principle or discovery, the thing from which the deduction is made must be sufficiently established to have gained general acceptance in the particular field in which it belongs.

We think the systolic blood pressure deception test has not yet gained such standing and scientific recognition among physiological and psychological authorities as would justify the courts in admitting expert testimony deduced from the discovery, development, and experiments thus far made.

The judgment is affirmed.

CASE STUDY Daubert v. Merrell Dow Pharmaceuticals, 509 U.S. 579 (1993)

In the 1950s, American doctors began prescribing an anti-nausea drug called Bendectin to pregnant women who were experiencing morning sickness. Bendectin was prescribed to more than 35 million American women between 1956 and 1983, when it was withdrawn from the market. The drug was manufactured by Merrell Dow Pharmaceutical Company. Several children of women who had taken Bendectin were born with serious birth defects, and their parents believed that the defects were caused by the drug.

Jason Daubert and Eric Schuller were two of the children who were born with serious birth defects. They and their parents sued Merrell Dow, alleging that their birth defects had been caused by their mothers' ingestion of Bendectin. The company moved for summary judgment, claiming that there was no admissible evidence that Bendectin caused birth defects. Merrell Dow submitted an affidavit from a well-credentialed physician epidemiologist, Steven H. Lamm. He stated that he had reviewed all the literature in the area – more than 30 published studies involving over 130,000 patients – and that no study had found Bendectin to be capable of causing birth defects. The plaintiffs submitted the testimony of eight well-credentialed experts of their own who testified that Bendectin can cause birth defects. Their conclusions were based upon animal studies, pharmacological studies of the chemical structure of Bendectin, and the reanalysis of some of the prior published epidemiological studies.

The trial judge applied the "general acceptance" *Frye* test, granted the motion for summary judgment, and dismissed the case. The judge held that plaintiffs' expert testimony based on animal studies and the recalculations of previous human study data was not admissible because it was not generally accepted and had not been published in professional journals. The plaintiffs appealed, but the Ninth Circuit Court of Appeals affirmed the ruling.

On further appeal, the Supreme Court held that the recently adopted Federal Rules of Evidence superseded and replaced the Frye "general acceptance" test. Rule 702 at that time stated:

> If scientific, technical, or other specialized knowledge will assist the trier of fact to understand the evidence or to determine a fact in issue, a witness qualified as an expert by knowledge, skill, experience, training, or education, may testify thereto in the form of an opinion or otherwise.

The Supreme Court stated:

> Nothing in the text of this Rule establishes "general acceptance" as an absolute prerequisite to admissibility. Nor does respondent present any clear indication that Rule 702 or the Rules as a whole were intended to incorporate a "general acceptance" standard. The drafting history makes no mention of *Frye,* and a rigid "general acceptance" requirement would be at odds with the "liberal thrust" of the Federal Rules and their "general approach of relaxing the traditional barriers to 'opinion' testimony."

and added:

> That the *Frye* test was displaced by the Rules of Evidence does not mean, however, that the Rules themselves place no limits on the admissibility of purportedly scientific evidence. Nor is the trial judge disabled from

> screening such evidence. To the contrary, under the Rules the trial judge must ensure that any and all scientific testimony or evidence admitted is not only relevant, but reliable.

Rather, the Court said that the judge must decide "whether the reasoning or methodology underlying the testimony is scientifically valid" and "whether that reasoning or methodology properly can be applied to the facts in issue." The court suggested several factors to be considered, including whether the reasoning and methodology have been or can be scientifically tested, its error rate, whether there are standards in the field, whether they have published in professional journals, and whether it has been generally accepted. Because the lower courts had not applied the proper test of admissibility, the Supreme Court sent the case back to them "for further proceedings consistent with this opinion."

The plaintiffs' victory in the Supreme Court was short-lived. On remand, rather than sending the case back to the trial court for a jury trial, the Ninth Circuit decided to reconsider its earlier opinion and apply what the authoring judge, Judge Kozinski, interpreted as the new Supreme Court test. Emphasizing the fact, not discussed by the Supreme Court, that the plaintiffs' expert evidence was prepared for litigation rather than being the result of benign research, he again affirmed the trial court's summary judgment for the pharmaceutical company. The Supreme Court refused to hear an appeal of that ruling. In spite of the Supreme Court's earlier decision, the result was that the plaintiffs were never allowed to have a jury decide whether their birth defects were caused by Bendectin.

REFERENCES

Daubert v. Merrell Dow Pharmaceuticals, Inc., 509 U.S. 579 (1993)

Daubert v. Merrell Dow Pharmaceuticals, Inc., 43 F.3d 1311 (9th Cir. 1995) on remand

Fed. R. Evid. 702

Frye v. United States, 54 App. D. C. 46, 293 F. 1013 (1923)

Funk, C., *Daubert vs. Frye: A State-by-State Comparison*, Expert Institute (July, 2024) https://www.expertinstitute.com/resources/insights/daubert-versus-frye-a-national-look-at-expert-evidentiary-standards/

General Electric Co. v. Joiner, 522 U.S. 136 (1997)

Kumho Tire Co., Ltd. v. Carmichael, 526 U.S. 137 (1999)

READINGS

Barnes, D., *General Acceptance Versus Scientific Soundness: Mad Scientists in the Courtroom*, 31 Fla. St. U. L. Rev. (2004) https://ir.law.fsu.edu/lr/vol31/iss2/4

Behrens, M. and Trask, A., *Federal Rule of Evidence 702: A History and Guide to the 2023 Amendments Governing Expert Evidence*, 12 Tex. A&M L. Rev. (2024–2025) https://scholarship.law.tamu.edu/lawreview/vol12/iss1/6/

Gomzales, L., *The Admissibility of Scientific Evidence: The History and Demise of Frye v. United States*, 48 Univ. Miami L. Rev. 371 (1993) https://repository.law.miami.edu/umlr/vol48/iss2/7/

Lepore, J., *On Evidence: Proving Frye as a Matter of Law, Science, and History*, 184 Yale L. J. 882 (215) https://www.yalelawjournal.org/essay/on-evidence-proving-frye-as-a-matter-of-law-science-and-history

National Institute of Justice, *The Slow but Steady March Towards a More Reliable Forensic Science*, U.S. Department of Justice (December 7, 2022) https://nij.ojp.gov/topics/articles/slow-steady-march-towards-more-reliable-forensic-science

Neufeld, P., *The (Near) Irrelevance of Daubert to Criminal Justice and Some Suggestions for Reform*, 95 Am. J. Public Health. S107–S113 (2011) https://doi.org/10.2105/AJPH.2004.056333

Smith, P., *Where Science Enters the Courtroom, the Daubert Name Looms Large*, Undark Magazine (2020) https://undark.org/2020/02/17/daubert-standard-joyce-jason/

Weiss, K., Watson, C. and Xuan, Y., *Frye's Backstory: A Tale of Murder, a Retracted Confession, and Scientific Hubris*, 42 J. Am. Acad. Psychiatry L. 42 (2014) https://jaapl.org/content/42/2/226

3

The Problem with Bad Science

The 20th century was marked by amazing developments in science and technology. Scientific advancements in physics, chemistry, and biology led to the development of quantum mechanics, nuclear weapons, new materials like plastics, and the near eradication of polio and other diseases. Technological advances in electricity, transportation, and communication gave us the light bulb, automobiles, airplanes, television, and early computers.

The use of science in the legal system followed those developments and the use of forensic science proliferated. There were significant changes as the investigation of crime moved from a total reliance on eyewitnesses to the use of scientific technologies and methods. Trace and pattern evidence analysis became the norm as police used fingerprints, hair, blood types, and other materials to connect a suspect to a crime scene. The dual microscope became a prime method for comparison of trace evidence samples. New techniques included ballistics and handwriting comparisons. The police built their own forensic science laboratories to develop and analyze evidence using these new techniques. Trials changed and prosecutors relied heavily on forensic science testimony to convince jurors of the defendant's guilt.

In the late twentieth and early 21st century, the discovery of deoxyribonucleic acid (DNA) would lead to the most important change in criminal justice in over 200 years. The discovery that a molecule of DNA carries all of the genetic information that passed from parent to child and that the molecule is present in virtually all the cells of the human body changed chemistry, biology, and medicine forever. It also changed the criminal justice system. The fact that DNA contains all of the information that makes an individual person different from almost every other person in the world was the ultimate identification tool. In 1984, Sir Alec Jeffreys,

DOI: 10.4324/9781041136361-4

a British geneticist, developed a system of DNA profiling that enabled forensic scientists to compare cells left at a crime scene, such as saliva, semen, blood, or hair, to that of a suspect and make an almost infallible conclusion about identity. The ability to extract and compare DNA has become even better with recent developments.

3.1 FORENSIC SCIENCE AND EXONERATIONS

DNA became recognized as the ultimate tool to identify the perpetrator of a crime. But DNA would also produce the evidence that would call into question the validity of several traditional forensic science techniques. DNA in criminal justice is a "double-edged sword" in the sense that as good as it is at identifying the person who left the evidence at the scene, it is equally good at identifying the person who did *not* leave that evidence. It is a valuable method to prove innocence as well as guilt. DNA thus became a primary tool for exonerating persons who had been wrongfully convicted based on other evidence (Garrett, 2009). As of April 2025, 3,659 convicted persons have been exonerated and proven to have been wrongfully convicted (National Registry of Exonerations, 2025). Equally important is the fact that for each of these exonerations a guilty person has still not been identified or caught and is still free to commit more crimes (Figure 3.1).

For forensic science, what is disturbing about these exonerations is that in almost a third of the exonerations, some form of forensic science was used to wrongfully convict them in the first place. 29%, over a thousand people, were convicted based on forensic evidence that we know was wrong. And 34% of the wrongful homicide convictions were based at least in part, on bad forensic evidence (National Registry of Exonerations, 2025).

3.2 THE NATIONAL ACADEMY OF SCIENCES REPORT

In 2005, exonerations and other concerns about the validity of forensic science as a tool for criminal justice led Congress to commission the National Academy of Sciences (NAS) to conduct a thorough study of the state of forensic science in the United States. Among other things, the NAS was charged to "disseminate best practices and guidelines concerning the collection and analysis of forensic evidence to help ensure quality and consistency in the use of forensic technologies and techniques to solve crimes, investigate deaths, and protect the public." (National Research Council, 2009). The NAS convened a

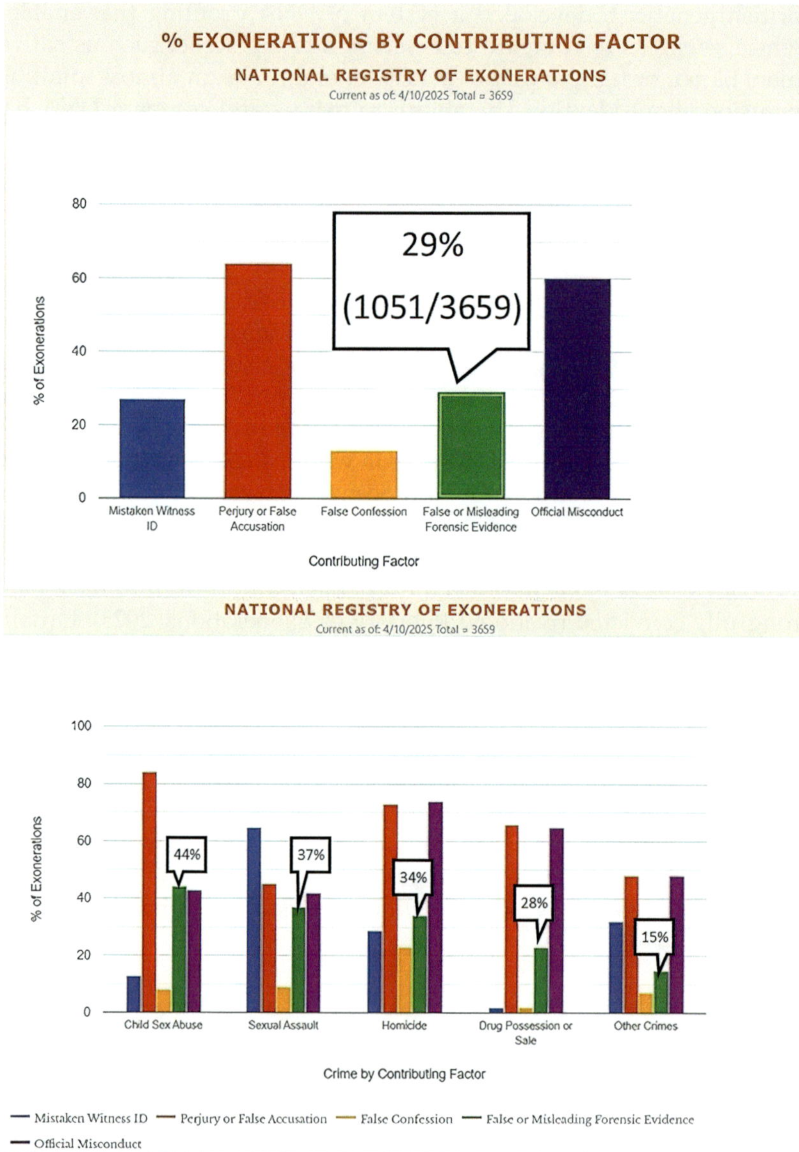

Figure 3.1 Exonerations by Contributing Factor.

Source: National Registry of Exonerations: public use permitted

large study group that included members of the forensic science community, members of the legal community, and a diverse group of scientists. After years of study, in 2009, the NAS submitted its lengthy report, titled "Strengthening Forensic Science in the United States: A Path Forward." The report addressed many forms of forensic science, including biological evidence, controlled substances, friction ridge analysis (fingerprints), shoeprints and tire tracks, toolmark and firearms identification, hair evidence, fiber evidence, questioned document examination (handwriting), paint and coatings evidence, explosives and fire debris, forensic odontology (bite marks), bloodstain patterns, and digital and multimedia analysis. The following chapters examine the details of the NAS Report in many of those areas. The basic conclusion of the NAS Report however was very disturbing. The NAS found that many of these forms of forensic science "lack validity." The report states:

NATIONAL ACADEMY OF SCIENCES

[W]ith the exception of nuclear DNA analysis . . . no forensic method has been rigorously shown to have the capacity to consistently, and with a high degree of certainty, demonstrate a connection between evidence and a specific individual or source.

The 350-page report found that many traditional forensic sciences lacked empirical evidence to support their courtroom claims of individualization or identification (Kaye, 2010). The report recommended that we "develop rigorous protocols to guide these subjective interpretations and pursue equally rigorous research and evaluation programs." The NAS Report also found that these rigorous protocols were not likely to be developed through the legal process. The report said that "the legal system is ill-equipped to correct the problems of the forensic science community." As discussed in the next chapter, the NAS committee was certainly right about that.

REFERENCES

Garrett, B. L. and Neufeld, P. J., *Invalid Forensic Science Testimony and Wrongful Convictions*, 95 Va. L. Rev. 1 (2009) https://scholarship.law.duke.edu/faculty_scholarship/3861/

Kaye, D., *The Good, the Bad, the Ugly: The NAS Report on Strengthening Forensic Science in America*, 50 Science & Justice 8 (March 2010) https://papers.ssrn.com/sol3/papers.cfm?abstract_id=1849165

National Registry of Exonerations (2025) https://exonerationregistry.org/

National Research Council of the National Academies of Science, *Strengthening Forensic Science in the United States: A Path Forward* (2009) https://nap.nationalacademies.org/catalog/12589/strengthening-forensic-science-in-the-united-states-a-path-forward

READINGS

Bonaventure, C., *Wrongful Convictions and Forensic Science*, Wires Forensic Science (December 22, 2020) https://doi.org/10.1002/wfs2.1406

Hill, T., *Close Enough for Government Work: The Use of "Junk Science" and Its Effect on Modern Policing*, 32 Cornell J. Law Public Policy (2022) https://community.lawschool.cornell.edu/wp-content/uploads/2023/09/Hill-note-final.pdf

Kovach, K., Colloff, P. and Murphy, B., *It Forensics or is It Junk Science?* Pro Publica (January 21, 2023) https://www.propublica.org/article/understanding-junk-science-forensics-criminal-justice

Servick, K., *Reversing the Legacy of Junk Science in the Courtroom*, Science (March 2016) https://www.science.org/content/article/reversing-legacy-junk-science-courtroom

Thompson, W., *Beyond Bad Apples: Analyzing the Role of Forensic Science in Wrongful Convictions*, 37 Sw. U. L. Rev. 1027 (2008) https://papers.ssrn.com/sol3/papers.cfm?abstract_id=2214465#

4

Science and the Law
Ships Passing in the Night

The prediction of the NAS Report about the inability of the legal system to make improvements to forensic science has unfortunately proven to be true. Our criminal justice system has not on the whole done much to prevent unscientific testimony. The adversarial system has not brought about a significant reduction in the use of unsubstantiated forensic science testimony in criminal cases. Prosecutors continue to offer traditional forms of forensic science testimony despite the reported lack of scientific validity. Defense lawyers rarely challenge such evidence. In those cases when it is challenged, judges rarely use their gatekeeping responsibility to exclude it and usually rely on the fact that it has been admitted in prior cases. The NAS Report found:

> [T]he vast majority of the *reported* opinions in criminal cases indicate that trial judges rarely exclude or restrict expert testimony offered by prosecutors; most *reported* opinions also indicate that appellate courts routinely deny appeals contesting trial court decisions admitting forensic evidence against criminal defendants.
>
> National Research Council (2009)

Why is there this disconnect between science and the law? Why do judges ignore scientific conclusions about faulty evidence that can, and does, lead to the conviction of innocent people? Why is there such a strong resistance to the findings in the NAS Report? Why do judges often refuse to even conduct a hearing and simply admit the old familiar forms of

DOI: 10.4324/9781041136361-5

forensic science evidence in spite of the serious questions about its validity? Part of the answer is that scientists and judges are both just doing what they were taught.

4.1 LEGAL TRAINING AND THE SCIENTIFIC METHOD

The scientific method is a search for knowledge and truth. It involves observation, questioning, forming a hypothesis, gathering data through experimentation, analyzing that data, and drawing conclusions. Scientists begin by observing a phenomenon and using instruments to gather information about it. They then formulate questions about the phenomenon and make a hypothesis, a tentative explanation or prediction that can be tested. Scientists then conduct experiments to test that hypothesis and collect data from those experiments. They analyze the data and draw conclusions about their hypothesis. Scientists usually communicate their findings in scientific journals so that other scientists in the field can review their work (Ryan, 2022).

The *Daubert* case in effect told judges to determine if the evidence being offered was the result of the application of this scientific method. Has it been tested? What did the experiments show about how many times it was substantiated in an error rate? Were the experiments standardized so they could be repeated by others? Has the theory been reviewed by other scientists in scientific publications? Do other scientists accept the theory behind the offered testimony? Those are the hallmarks of validity that judges are to use in performing their evidence gatekeeping function.

On the other hand, American legal training is based on a premise that is totally different from the scientific method. The law values stability. Lawyers and judges are trained to use the concept of precedent and *stare decisis* – that the answer to present questions can always be found by looking to the past. In law school, they use "case books" rather than textbooks. For every legal issue, lawyers are taught not to seek the answer objectively based on the available information but rather to simply ask how judges have answered the question in the past. That is how lawyers learn. When lawyers become judges, they utilize the same method that they were taught and that they honed as practicing attorneys.

The use of precedent to decide an issue is based on the legal concept of "stare decisis," a Latin phrase that translates to "stand by things decided." According to this doctrine, judges should follow the decisions of judges in previous cases when deciding similar issues. There are reasons for the law's reliance on precedent. It fosters stability and predictability. The doctrine is usually justified by arguments which focus on the desirability of certainty in the law and also by notions of justice and fairness. Benjamin Cardozo, in his treatise, *The Nature of the Judicial Process*, stated:

> It will not do to decide the same question one way between one set of litigants and the opposite way between another. "If a group of cases involves the same point, the parties expect the same decision. It would be a gross injustice to decide alternate cases on opposite principles. . . ." Adherence to precedent must then be the rule rather than the exception if litigants are to have faith in the even-handed administration of justice in the courts.
>
> Cardozo (1921) at p. 9

In other words, the law is always biased in favor of the status quo, not because it is the correct result but because it is the status quo and should not be disturbed. One commentator described it:

> Stare decisis – reasoning from precedent – requires adhering to a prior decision because it is the prior decision, not necessarily because it is correct. . . . We are cognitively primed to subconsciously prefer precedent – and then, instead of correcting that bias, we built a legal system that requires courts to follow precedent.
>
> Jois (2009) at p. 96

Even courts that still apply the *Frye* standard of general acceptance rather than a *Daubert* analysis misinterpret *Frye* to mean "general acceptance in the legal community" rather than what *Frye* said was "general acceptance in the relevant scientific community." And some State *Frye* courts have even limited any general acceptance review to "new or novel" forensic sciences (Figures 4.1–4.5). In other words, if they have admitted it in the past, no further analysis is required [People v. Basler, 740 N.E.2d 1 (Ill. Sup. Ct. 2000)].

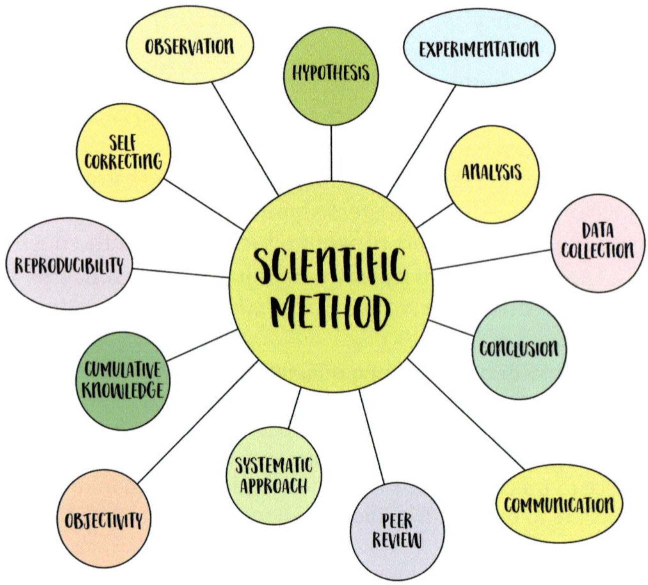

Figure 4.1 The Scientific Method as an Ongoing Process.

Source: iStock

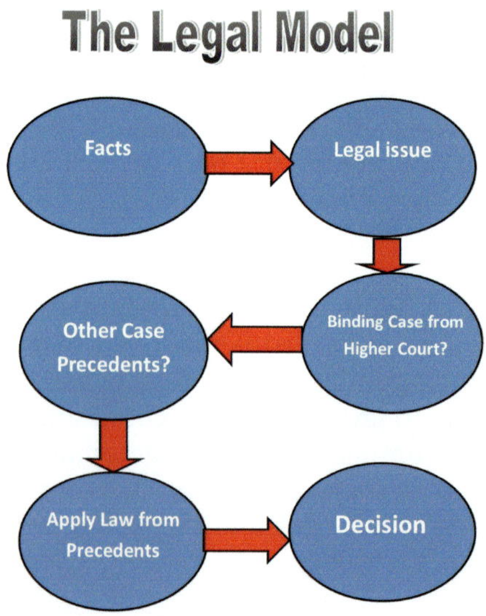

Figure 4.2 The Legal Model.

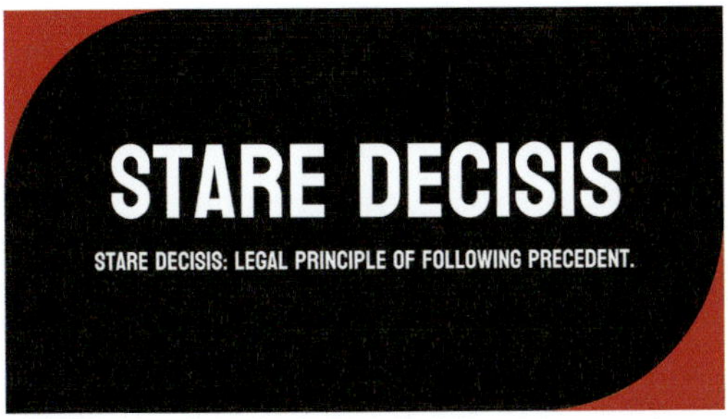

Figure 4.3 Stare Decisis.

Source: Shutterstock

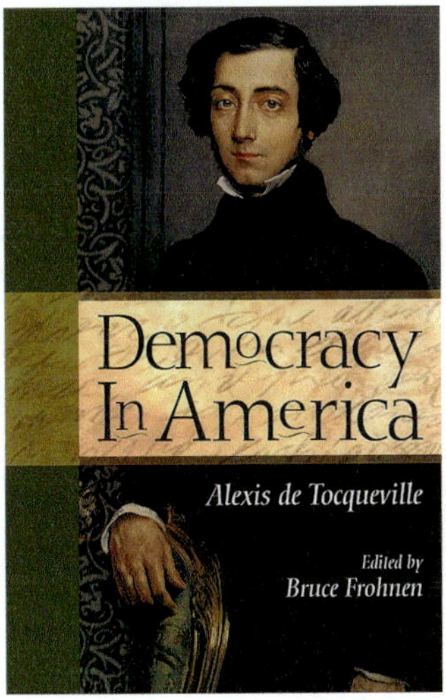

Figure 4.4 Democracy in America.

Americans have retained the law of precedents; that is to say, they continue to found their legal opinions and the decisions of their courts upon the opinions and decisions of their predecessors. In the mind of an English or American lawyer a taste and a reverence for what is old is almost always united with a love of regular and lawful.

Alexis de Tocqueville, "Democracy in America" 1838.

Figure 4.5 The Path of the Law.

> It is revolting to have no better reason for a rule of law than that it was laid down in the time of Henry IV. It is still more revolting if the grounds upon which it was laid down have vanished long since, and the rule simply persists from blind imitation of the past.
>
> Oliver Wendell Holmes Jr., "The Path of Law", 1897

4.2 PRECEDENT AND FORENSIC SCIENCE

When science tries to come into the courtroom, it comes into the direct path of the judicial system's reliance on precedent, even in federal courts where the Supreme Court has directed judges to apply the *Daubert* tests for admissibility. *United States v. Crisp*, 324 F.3d 261 (4th Cir. 2003), is a classic example.

After a jury trial, Crisp was convicted of bank robbery, bank robbery with a dangerous weapon, and a firearm offense. He was sentenced to over 21 years in prison. The conviction was based in part on the testimony of a police fingerprint analyst that Crisp's fingerprints matched a palm print on an incriminating note he had allegedly written to a coconspirator in the jail. A police handwriting expert also testified that Crisp's handwriting matched that on the same note. On appeal, Crisp challenged the admissibility of both fingerprint and handwriting analysis.

As to the fingerprints, Crisp made a *Daubert* argument:

> [T]the premises underlying fingerprinting evidence have not been adequately tested, . . . that there is no known rate of error for latent fingerprint identifications, that fingerprint examiners operate without a uniform threshold of certainty required for a positive identification, and that fingerprint evidence has not achieved general acceptance in the relevant scientific community.
>
> U.S. v. Crisp (2003) at p. 266

As to the handwriting testimony, Crisp made a similar *Daubert* argument:

> [L]ike fingerprinting identifications, the basic premise behind handwriting analysis is that no two persons write alike, and thus that forensic document examiners can reliably determine authorship of a particular document by comparing it with known samples. He maintains that these basic premises have not been tested, nor has an error rate been established. In addition, he asserts that handwriting experts have no numerical standards to govern their analyses and that they have not subjected themselves and their science to critical self-examination and study.
>
> U.S. v. Crisp (2003) at p. 270

There was no *Daubert* hearing in the trial court, but the appeals court did not care, saying, "Under Daubert, a trial judge need not expend scarce judicial resources reexamining a familiar form of expertise every time opinion evidence is offered." U.S. v. Crisp (2003) at p. 268. The appeals court did what judges are trained to do and relied on past court decisions in denying Crisp's appeal, saying, "Crisp today advocates the wholesale exclusion of a long-accepted form of expert evidence. Such a drastic step is not required of us under Daubert, however, and we decline to take it." U.S. v. Crisp (2003) at p. 268. Instead of requiring a *Daubert* hearing to address the validity of fingerprinting and handwriting analysis, the *Crisp* court just cited other court opinions where judges had discussed similar testimony.

One of the appeals judges dissented:

> The majority believes that expert testimony about fingerprint and handwriting identification is reliable because the techniques in these fields have been accepted and tested in our adversarial system over time. This belief leads the majority to excuse fingerprint and handwriting analysis from the more scrutiny that scientific expert testimony must now withstand under Daubert . . . before it can be admitted. In Patrick Leroy Crisp's case the government did not prove that its expert identification evidence satisfied the Daubert factors or that it was otherwise reliable. . . . I am not suggesting that fingerprint and handwriting evidence cannot be shown to satisfy Daubert. I am only making the point that the government did not establish in Crisp's case that this evidence is reliable. The government has had ten years to comply with Daubert. It should not be given a pass in this case.
>
> U.S. v. Crisp (2003) at p. 272

4.3 THE BURDEN OF PROOF AND JURY DEFERENCE

The *Crisp* decision also demonstrates how some courts have changed what the law calls the "burden of proof" when they analyze challenges to traditional forms of forensic science evidence. Burden of proof means that the person making a claim is the one who must present evidence to establish that claim. When it comes to admitting evidence, the burden of proof is always on the party that wants to admit the evidence, known as the proponent, as opposed to the opponent. This requirement applies to the admission of all evidence. In a criminal case, when the government wants the jury to see or hear evidence, the prosecutor must prove to the judge that the evidence is admissible. For forensic science, this means that the prosecutor must prove that the expert testimony meets the requirements of *Daubert* or *Frye*, depending on the jurisdiction.

And yet, the *Crisp* court turned the rule upside down and put the burden on Crisp:

> Put simply, *Crisp has provided us no reason* today to believe that this general acceptance of the principles underlying fingerprint identification has, for decades, been misplaced.

and:

> But in light of *Crisp's failure to offer us any reason* today to doubt the reliability of handwriting analysis evidence in general, we must decline to deny our courts and juries such insights as it can offer.
>
> U.S. v. Crisp (2003) at p. 269 (emphasis added)

The *Crisp* opinion provides another example of how some courts have rationalized the admission of traditional forms of forensic science evidence. They simply say that they will leave it to the jury to decide whether to believe the expert testimony. The *Crisp* court said, "To the extent that a given handwriting analysis is flawed or flimsy, an able defense lawyer will bring that fact to the jury's attention, both through skillful cross-examination and by presenting expert testimony of his own." Crisp v. U.S. (2003) at p. 271. The basic error in this proposition is that it ignores the responsibility of the judge to protect the jury from unreliable evidence, which is the heart of admissibility. This is especially important when it comes to expert testimony. Once the judge allows a person to testify and give opinions as an "expert," the jurors assume that the witness is a credible witness who has special expertise that they should rely on. It is also known as the "white coat syndrome," where jurors defer to admitted evidence from "experts," rather than critically evaluating the evidence they present.

4.4 AMENDMENTS TO FRE 702

The *Crisp* case is just an example, and it is not the exception. One study found:

> A recent study was conducted to see if judges were following FRE 702. Contrary to basic rules of evidence, they put the burden of the opponent of the evidence rather than the proponent. In 2020, there were 1,059 federal cases in which the trial judge admitted, partially admitted, or denied expert testimony. In approximately 35% of the cases (373), the trial judge required the proponent to prove the admissibility of the expert evidence by a preponderance of the evidence. In almost two-thirds

> of the cases – 65% (686 of 1059) – the trial judge did not mention the preponderance standard at all. About 13% of the time (135 cases), the judge described the analysis under Rule 702 or *Daubert* as having a "liberal thrust," employed a "liberal policy favoring admissibility," or stated that "exclusion is the exception rather than the rule" – contrary to the requirement of Rules 702 and 104(a) that the proponent must prove the admissibility of the proffered expert testimony by a preponderance of the evidence. Jackson (2021)

A Supreme Court committee looked at the issue and recommended changes because:

> Finally, the Committee resolved to respond to the fact that many courts have declared that the reliability requirements set forth in Rule 702(b) and (d) – that the expert has relied on sufficient facts or data and has reliably applied a reliable methodology – are questions of weight and not admissibility, and more broadly that expert testimony is presumed to be admissible. These statements misstate Rule 702, because its admissibility requirements must be established to a court by a preponderance of the evidence. The Committee concluded that in a fair number of cases, the courts have found expert testimony admissible even though the proponent has not satisfied the Rule 702(b) and (d) requirements by a preponderance of the evidence – essentially treating these questions as ones of weight rather than admissibility, which is contrary to the Supreme Court's holdings that under Rule 104(a), admissibility requirements are to be determined by court under the preponderance standard.
>
> Report of the Advisory Committee (2002) at p. 6

After nearly 30 years of opinions similar to Crisp, the Supreme Court amended Federal Rule of Evidence 702 to address these issues. In December 2023, FRE 702 was amended to add clarifying language:

RULE 702 TESTIMONY BY EXPERT WITNESSES (EFFECTIVE DECEMBER 2023)

A witness who is qualified as an expert by knowledge, skill, experience, training, or education may testify in the form of an opinion or otherwise if *the proponent demonstrates to the court that it is more likely than not that*

(a) the expert's scientific, technical, or other specialized knowledge will help the trier of fact to understand the evidence or to determine a fact in issue;
(b) the testimony is based on sufficient facts or data;
(c) the testimony is the product of reliable principles and methods;
(d) the expert's *opinion reflects a reliable application* of the principles and methods to the facts of the case.

These changes are significant. First, the rule now clearly places the burden on the *proponent* (the person who offers the evidence) of the evidence to establish its reliability. Second, it clearly states that the proof of reliability must be demonstrated *to the court* and not left to the jury. Third, it sets the burden of proof as *more likely than not* – the familiar preponderance standard. Finally, it clarifies that the judge must find that the expert's testimony is not only based on reliable science but also that the expert has *reliably applied* that science to the issue in the case. However, it is important to remember that the Rule only technically applies in federal cases. States will still need to decide whether their State rules will be similarly amended.

CASE STUDY United States v. Crisp, 324 F.3d 261 (4th Cir. 2003)

"DON'T WRITE NOTES IN JAIL!"

At approximately 12:25 p.m. on June 13, 2001, a lone male, wearing a mask and surgical gloves, and carrying a handgun, entered the Central Carolina Bank in Durham, North Carolina. He approached Joan Adams, a teller, threw a bag on the counter, and instructed her to "fill up the god*mned f* * *ing bag." Adams promptly gave the gunman the sum of $7,854 in cash, which included bait bills and an electronic tracking device. Then, a horn sounded twice from the parking lot outside, and the robber left the bank and made his getaway in a purple Ford Probe automobile. The next day, June 14, 2001, the authorities received a call on its Crimestoppers telephone line from an individual who claimed to have information about the robbery of the Central Carolina Bank. The caller provided detailed information, and later that day the police met the caller, Michael Mitchell, at a local restaurant. Mitchell informed the officers that Patrick Crisp and Lamont Torain had robbed the bank. He further attested that Crisp and Torain had attempted to recruit him to participate in the robbery, but that he had declined. Mitchell explained that Crisp had detailed the entire robbery plan to him. On the basis of Mitchell's information, the police obtained an arrest warrant for Crisp.

On June 15, 2001, Crisp, while driving a rented Pontiac Grand Am with Mitchell as a passenger, came upon a police license checkpoint. Crisp was unable to produce a valid driver's license, and he advised the officers that his name was Jermaine Jackson. A small amount of marijuana was found in the vehicle. While *Crisp* was being interviewed, Mitchell informed the police of Crisp's real identity, and the officers promptly learned of the outstanding warrant for Crisp's arrest. Crisp was then taken into custody. Torain was also arrested, and he was incarcerated in the same jail as Crisp. On June 20, 2001, as he walked past Crisp's cell, a handwritten note (the "Note") was slid out from under Crisp's door. The Note, the last line of which was allegedly crossed out when delivered, stated:

> Lamont
>
> You know if you don't help me I am going to get life in prison, and you ain't going to get nothing. Really it's over for me if you don't change what you told them.
>
> Tell them I picked you up down the street in Kathy's car. Tell them that I don't drive the Probe. Tell them Mike drove the Probe. He is the one that told on us. Tell them the gun and all that shit was Mike's. That is what I am going to tell them tommorow [sic].
>
> Tell the Feds Mike drove you away from the bank.
>
> Patrick.

> At trial, Mary Katherine Brannan, a fingerprint expert with the North Carolina State Bureau of Investigation ("SBI"), testified that Crisp's right palm had produced a latent print that had subsequently been recovered from the Note. Furthermore, a handwriting expert, Special Agent Thomas Currin, a "questioned document analyst" with the SBI, testified that Crisp had authored the Note. . . . After the four-day jury trial, Crisp was found guilty of bank robbery, bank robbery with a dangerous weapon, and brandishing a firearm during and in relation to the bank robbery.

REFERENCES

Cardozo, B., *The Nature of the Judicial Process* (1921). Yale University Press.

Fed. R. Evid. 702

Holmes Jr., O. W., *The Path of Law*, 10 Harv. L. Rev. 457 (1897) https://facultyweb.cortland.edu/ocallaghan/pdf/Holmes.pdf

Jackson, K. and Trask, A., *Federal Rule of Evidence 702: A One Year Review and Study of Decisions in 2020*, Lawyers for Civil Justice (2021) www.lfcj.com/document-directory/federal-rule-of-evidence-702a-one-year-review-and-study-of-decisions-in-2020

Jois, G., *Stare Decisis in Cognitive Error*, 75 Brook. L. Rev. (2009)

People v. Basler, 740 N.E.2d 1 (Ill. Sup. Ct. 2000)

Report of the Advisory Committee on Evidence Rules, Judicial Conference of the United States (2022) www.uscourts.gov/file/43957/download

Ryan, M. and O'Callaghan, A., *The Scientific Method*, Reno, Extension | University of Nevada, FS-02-66 (2022) https://extension.unr.edu/publication.aspx?PubID=4239

Tocqueville, A. de., *Democracy in America* (2000), H. C. Mansfield & D. Winthrop, Trans. University of Chicago Press.

READINGS

Alexander, L., *Constrained by Precedent*, 63 S. Cal. L. Rev. 1 (1989) https://heinonline.org/HOL/Page?collection=journals&handle=hein.journals/scal63&id=15&men_tab=srchresults

Capurso, T., *How Judges Judge: Theories on Judicial Decision Making*, 29 U. Balt. L. F. (1999) https://scholarworks.law.ubalt.edu/cgi/viewcontent.cgi?article=1909&context=lf

Douglas, W., *Stare Decisis*, 49 Colum. L. Rev. 735 (1949) https://www.jstor.org/stable/111914

Haack, S., *Irreconcilable Differences? The Troubled Marriage of Science and Law*, 72 Law Contemp. Probl. 1 (Winter 2009) https://scholarship.law.duke.edu/lcp/vol72/iss1/2

Kirk, P., *The Interrelationship of Law and Science*, 13 Buff. L. Rev. 393 (1964) https://digitalcommons.law.buffalo.edu/buffalolawreview/vol13/iss2/11

Martin, B., Law *Versus Science*, chapter in *Groupthink in Science: Greed, Pathological Altruism, Ideology, Competition, and Culture*, Allen, D. and Howell, J. (Eds.) (2020), pp. 115–126. Springer. https://www.bmartin.cc/pubs/20Allen-law-science.html

Sloan, L. and Berger, M., *The Uneasy Relationship Between Science and Law: An Essay and Introduction*, 73 Brook. L. Rev. 847 (2008) https://brooklynworks.brooklaw.edu/cgi/viewcontent.cgi?referer=&httpsredir=1&article=1276&context=faculty

Part II

The Reliability of Pattern Identifications

5

Generalization and Individualization

Television shows about forensic science, like the "CSI" television franchise, often feature a scene or maybe a teaser where a laboratory technician in a white coat proclaims, "It's a match!" It is not just in the media. For years, traditional forensic science witnesses have used terms like "match" or "reasonable degree of scientific certainty" or "cannot be excluded" when explaining their conclusions to a jury. And such phrases can have a profound impact on a jury. For example, studies have shown that the likelihood of a guilty verdict increases dramatically when the expert witness testifies that some trace evidence, such as fingerprints, handwriting, or a gun cartridge, for instance, "matches" a sample from the defendant or a gun associated with the defendant (Mcquiston, 2009). Also, lawyers who present forensic science testimony will often triumphantly ask the witness if their opinion is to a "reasonable degree of scientific certainty." The phrase, like the "match" phrase, has been a staple in court for decades. The witness and the lawyer are trying to convey to the jury that the opinion is based on sound science instead of a conjecture or estimate. But what do these phrases really mean in a scientific sense?

The NAS Report explicitly discouraged the use of such terms:

> There is a critical need in most fields of forensic science to raise the standards for reporting and testifying about the results of investigations. For example, many terms are used by forensic examiners in reports and in court testimony to describe findings, conclusions, and the degrees of association between evidentiary material (e.g., hairs, fingerprints, fibers) and particular

DOI: 10.4324/9781041136361-7

> people or objects. Such terms include but are not limited to "match," "consistent with," "identical," "similar in all respects tested," and "cannot be excluded as the source of." The use of such terms can have a profound effect on how the trier of fact in a criminal or civil matter perceives and evaluates evidence. Yet the forensic science disciplines have not reached agreement or consensus on the precise meaning of any of these terms.
>
> National Research Council (2009) at p. 185

5.1 "CERTAINTY," "MATCH," AND PROBABILITY

The scientific reality is that no comparison of samples can result in 100% certainty. Using the term "match" implies, and is interpreted by jurors to mean, that there is no other person in the world who would have the same characteristics. This fallacy was applied for years to pattern identifications, such as fingerprint or hair or handwriting comparison. For years, fingerprint examiners testified that "no two people in the world have the same fingerprints." This is a claim of uniqueness that no scientist can attest to. To say that it is true because they have never found one is the opposite of science. Difficult empirical research would be needed to establish that any of these impressions are unique. Instead, some experts state that there is uniqueness, inferring that a match then proves that the mark must have come from the source. Such reasoning is circular.

Similarly, "certainty" claims are not scientifically based and are a product of legal jargon. In 2016, the FBI directed its forensic scientists not to use the phrase "reasonable degree of certainty" in describing their conclusions. The Directory stated:

> Department forensic laboratories will review their policies and procedures to ensure that forensic examiners are not using the expressions "reasonable scientific certainty" or "reasonable [forensic discipline] certainty" in their reports or testimony. Department prosecutors will abstain from use of these expressions when presenting forensic reports or questioning forensic experts in court unless required by a judge or applicable law.
>
> U.S. Department of Justice, 2016

Why would the FBI take such a position? The phrase has no definition from a scientific perspective and is not a standard applied to peer-reviewed scientific journals. It is simply not a phrase that is accepted in scientific practice. The Federal Rules of Evidence do not mention it. Nevertheless, some States still seem to require it as a condition for the admission of expert testimony.

How then should scientific conclusions be expressed? The scientifically based answer is that, if possible, it should be expressed in terms of probability or likelihood based on available data.

5.2 STATISTICS, PROBABILITY, AND LIKELIHOOD

> Forensic science is undergoing an evolution in which a long-standing "trust the examiner" focus is being replaced by a "trust the scientific method" focus. This shift, which is in progress and still partial, is critical to ensure that the legal system uses forensic information in an accurate and valid way. Koehler (2023)

Forensic science is becoming more reliant on quantitative analysis to validate evidence. The fields of probability and statistics provide critical tools in that process. Statistics in the forensic setting are based on the collection and analysis of data. Probability is the likelihood that an event will occur based on an adequate set data.

When a witness discussing impression evidence says that something is "unique," they are claiming that the probability of finding another person or object with the same characteristics is zero. The problem is that there is no statistical data that supports such a conclusion. For example, to support the claim that a fingerprint is "unique" and that therefore only the defendant could have left that impression, there would have to be a database of the fingerprint on everyone in the world. Of course, that does not exist. But witnesses like to say that the proof of uniqueness is that they have never found two identical fingerprints. Despite the questionable basis for that statement, the problem is that such a statement proves nothing. The NAS Report included this example of vacuous reasoning:

> In most forensic science disciplines, no studies have been conducted of large populations to establish the uniqueness of marks or features. Yet, despite the lack of a statistical foundation, examiners make probabilistic claims based on their experience. . . . As Karl Popper famously explained, it is logically impossible to prove a hypothesis by accumulating positive instances. The hypothesis, "all swans are white," remains unproven, even after a large number of sightings of white swans, because the sighting of a single black swan would disprove it. Similarly, the hypothesis that no two objects are indistinguishably alike cannot be proven true from an accumulation of observations in which different object sources produce

distinctive markings. Even a very large number of pairwise, case-by-case comparisons made by individual examiners would not provide a satisfactory method for testing the object uniqueness claim.

National Research Council (2009) at p. 189

It is impossible to prove any human characteristic to be distinct in each individual without checking every individual, which has not been done. Balding (2015)

Without a database that includes every human, any conclusion about the likelihood that the defendant has the same characteristics (fingerprint, DNA, handwriting, etc.) as the crime scene sample is a probability not a certainty. The validity of the probability conclusion rests in part on the size of the database.

5.3 PROBABILITY IN FORENSIC ANALYSIS

Probability is the chance of a particular event happening. The likelihood ratio is the ratio of two probabilities of the same event under different hypotheses. The best example is what has become the standard for testimony about DNA profiling. Reputable DNA experts will never testify that the DNA crime scene sample came from the defendant or that the defendant's DNA "matches" the crime scene DNA. Rather, a DNA expert will testify about the likelihood of finding a person other than the defendant in the population with the same DNA characteristics as the crime scene DNA. We will discuss this in more detail in the chapter on DNA. The point is that this is probabilistic testimony, not the individualization fallacy. Probability testimony is a much more accurate way to convey to the jury the relative importance, or what lawyers call probative value, of forensic science testimony. Professors Saks and Koehler discussed the DNA approach and concluded in 2008:

Similar procedures, in principle, can be employed for other materials of forensic interest: fingerprints, handwriting, bitemarks, toolmarks, and so on. Criminalists face two challenges in developing such procedures. One challenge will be developing valid and reliable measures of the images of interest-of friction ridges, of toolmark striations, of bitemarks, of writing. A second challenge will be developing databases that identify the frequency with which various images appear. In some areas (e.g., toolmarks, firearms, and shoeprints), the challenge of producing sound probability estimates may be especially difficult because the materials change over time and with use. Saks (2008).

As explained in the succeeding chapters, some forensic science disciplines have made strides to develop databases that will support probabilistic testimony and others not so much.

REFERENCES

Balding, D., *Weight-of-Evidence for Forensic DNA Profiles* (2015). Wiley.

Koehler, J., et al., *The Scientific Reinvention of Forensic Science*, Proc Natl Acad Sci USA. (2023) www.pnas.org/doi/10.1073/pnas.2301840120

Mcquiston, D. and Saks, M., *The Testimony of Forensic Identification Science: What Expert Witnesses Say and What Factfinders Hear*, 33 Law Hum Behav. 436–453 (2009) https://www.researchgate.net/publication/24175922_The_Testimony_of_Forensic_Identification_Science_What_Expert_Witnesses_Say_and_What_Factfinders_Hear

National Research Council of the National Academies of Science, *Strengthening Forensic Science in the United States: A Path Forward* (2009), p. 185. https://nap.nationalacademies.org/catalog/12589/strengthening-forensic-science-in-the-united-states-a-path-forward

Saks, M. and Koehler, J., *The Individualization Fallacy in Forensic Science Evidence*, 91 Vanderbilt Law Rev. 199 (2008) https://scholarship.law.vanderbilt.edu/cgi/viewcontent.cgi?article=1492&context=vlr

U.S. Department of Justice, *Justice Department Announces New Steps to Advance and Strengthen Forensic Science* (September 12, 2016) https://www.justice.gov/archives/opa/pr/justice-department-announces-new-steps-advance-and-strengthen-forensic-science

READINGS

Kaye, D., *Probability, Individualization, and Uniqueness in Forensic Science Evidence: Listening to the Academies*, 75 Brook. L. Rev. 1163 (2010) https://brooklynworks.brooklaw.edu/blr/vol75/iss4/8

Lichtblau, E., *Justice Dept. to Tighten Rules on Testimony by Scientists*, New York Times (June 3, 2016) https://www.nytimes.com/2016/06/04/us/justice-dept-fbi-scientist-forensic-test.html

Saks, M. and Koehler, J., *The Individualization Fallacy in Forensic Science Evidence*, 91 Vanderbilt Law Review 199 (2008) https://scholarship.law.vanderbilt.edu/cgi/viewcontent.cgi?article=1492&context=vlr

Skene, P., *Up to the Courts: Managing Forensic Testimony with Limited Scientific Validity*, 102 Judicature (2018) https://judicature.duke.edu/articles/up-to-the-courts-managing-forensic-testimony-with-limited-scientific-validity/

Swofford, H. and Champod, C., *Probabilistic Reporting and Algorithms in Forensic Science: Stakeholder Perspectives within the American Criminal Justice System*, 4 Forensic Sci. Int. Synerg. (2022) https://www.sciencedirect.com/science/article/pii/S2589871X22000055

6

DNA

6.1 SOME BASICS ABOUT HEREDITY, GENETICS, AND DNA

An amateur orchardist has a hobby that is an interesting way to introduce some basic concepts of DNA (Figure 6.1).

If you take a Red Delicious apple, pull out and plant the seed, an apple tree will grow. What kind of apple will grow on that tree? If you said Red Delicious, let me ask you – do you look just like your mother? Of course not. You are half like your mother and half like your father. The apple seed is the same thing. Its mother was the Red Delicious tree it grew on. But its father was whatever kind of apple tree the bee stopped on before it pollinated the flower that turned into this seed. The result of that pollination is the seed. It is a ½ Red Delicious mother and ½ another apple variety father. Human genetics are the result of that same inherited combination of traits.

Like the apples, inherited human traits are passed down in a molecule of DNA that is in the nucleus of virtually every cell in the human body. The cell from the father's sperm combines with the cell from the mother's egg and that combined DNA is in every cell of the offspring's body. With the exception of identical twins, the resulting combination of DNA is unique in every human, at least as far as we know.

The history of the discovery of DNA was not related to the criminal justice system but grew out of pure biological research. James Watson and Francis Crick discovered that the structure of the DNA molecule was a

DOI: 10.4324/9781041136361-8

Figure 6.1 Honeybee Pollinating an Apple Blossom.

Source: Washington State University

double helix, connected by four chemical bases, or nucleotides, called adenine (A), guanine (G), cytosine (C), and thymine (T) (Figure 6.2).

DNA contains the instructions in the form of the myriad of combinations of the four nucleotides. These are the instructions for how the body develops. Each DNA sequence that contains these instructions is known as a gene. The complete system of DNA instructions is called the genome and the human genome contains about 3 billion bases and about 20,000 genes on 23 pairs of chromosomes.

The DNA double helix is a winding, two-stranded chemical structure. The shape gives DNA the power to pass along biological instructions with great precision. This unique structure also enables the molecule to copy itself every time a cell divides into more cells. The DNA helix splits and becomes two strands that go on to build two new, double-stranded DNA molecules in the new cells. Those cells go on to combine to form tissues, which form organs, and eventually the entire human organism. Although 99.9% of human DNA is the same, there are enough differences in the remaining sequences that we can identify one individual from another, unless they are identical twins. To do that we need to be able to develop a profile of those differences.

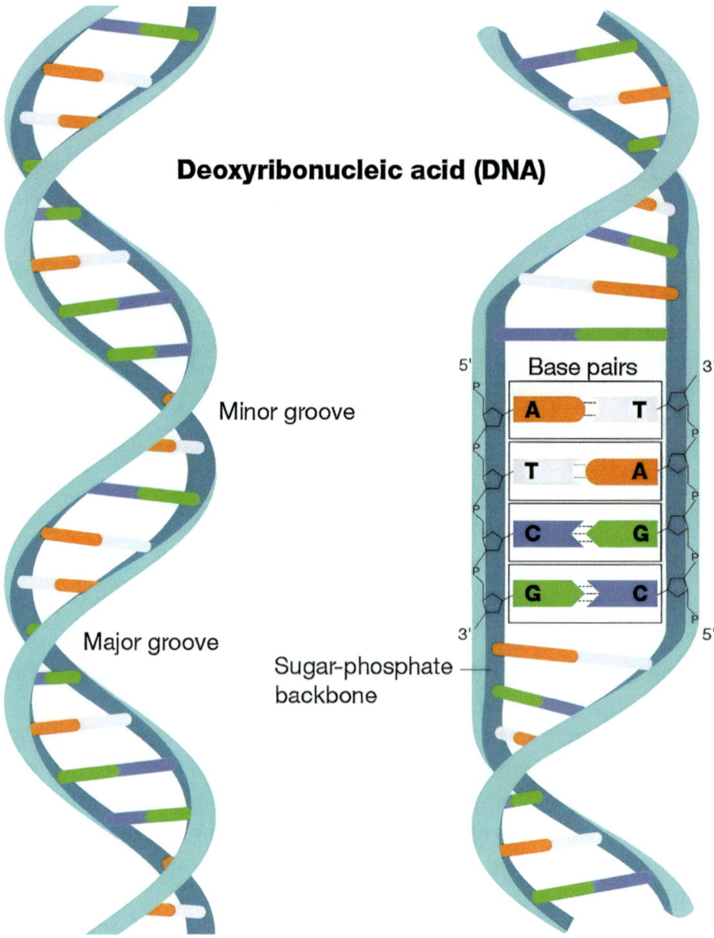

Figure 6.2 The DNA Molecule Double Helix.

Source: National Institute of Health

6.2 DNA PROFILING

Although most human DNA is the same, specific regions are different and are known as polymorphisms. If we can analyze these DNA polymorphisms, we can get a profile of the individual's DNA. In 1984, British geneticist Sir Alec Jeffreys developed a process to identify a person's DNA profile and to compare that profile to a sample of another person's DNA. His discovery led to the first use of DNA profiling in a criminal case.

The discovery and use of DNA profiling is without doubt the most important development in forensic science, and indeed in criminal justice, in over 200 years. The NAS Report described the impact of DNA:

> Although the forensic use of nuclear DNA is barely 20 years old, DNA typing is now universally recognized as the standard against which many other forensic individualization techniques are judged. DNA enjoys this preeminent position because of its reliability and the fact that, absent fraud or an error in labeling or handling, the probabilities of a false positive are quantifiable and often miniscule. However, even a very small (but nonzero) probability of false positive can affect the odds that a suspect is the source of a sample with a matching DNA profile. The scientific bases and reliability of other types of biological analysis are also well established, but absent nuclear DNA, they can only narrow the field of suspects, not suggest any particular individual.
>
> National Research Council (2009) at p. 130

> The past decade has seen great advances in a powerful criminal justice tool: deoxyribonucleic acid, or DNA. DNA can be used to identify criminals with incredible accuracy when biological evidence exists. By the same token, DNA can be used to clear suspects and exonerate persons mistakenly accused or convicted of crimes. In all, DNA technology is increasingly vital to ensuring accuracy and fairness in the criminal justice system.
>
> *U.S. Department of Justice (n.d.)*

Because DNA is in the nucleus of every cell in our body, it may be found and examined wherever human cells may be found, not only within our body but also on anything where we leave samples of those cells, whether it is blood, saliva, semen, sweat, hair with roots, skin cells left under a fingernail, or even in the latest DNA techniques maybe on anything we touch. Any of these things at a crime scene can be examined to detect and identify DNA. For comparison purposes, the DNA of an arrested person can be obtained by taking a sample of their cells. This is usually done by taking a sample of cheek cells with a cotton swab, called a buccal swab (Figure 6.3).

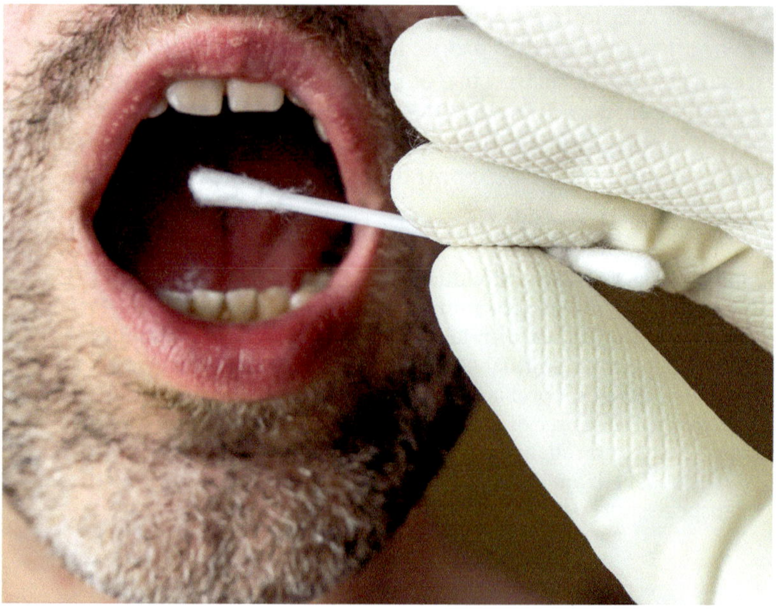

Figure 6.3 Taking a Buccal Swab.

Source: iStock

The process of DNA profiling has advanced greatly since Jeffreys' discovery. Before DNA can be analyzed, it must be extracted and purified. After that it can be amplified and a process called polymerase chain reaction (PCR) does that. PCR can amplify even small fragments of degraded DNA samples. Using PCR, a system called short tandem repeat (STR) is used to evaluate specific regions of the DNA. The true power of STR analysis is its ability to discriminate with statistical accuracy between one sample and another (National Institute of Justice, 2011).

More recently, some forensic scientists have developed the use of single nucleotide polymorphisms (SNPs) to establish a profile from even smaller and more degraded samples. An SNP is a common type of genetic variation where one DNA element differs between individuals. It is a substitution of a single nucleotide (A, T, C, or G) in a person's DNA sequence. Comparing these variations in two DNA samples can result in extremely accurate identifications, especially when there is a small quantity sample or a sample of low quality (Pedroza, 2025). Although STRs are the most prevalent method of DNA profiling, SNPs are additional genetic markers for even more precise human identity determination. Because of its cost and complexity, it is unlikely in the short run that SNP typing will replace STRs as the principal forensic method of human identification, but it is a valuable advancement that is becoming more common.

6.3 DNA DATABASES

6.3.1 The Human Genome Project

The Human Genome Project began in 1990, with the goal to map and sequence the entire human genome of approximately 3 billion DNA base pairs. The idea was to create a public database of genetic information about human DNA. It was completed in 2003 and revolutionized medicine to help researchers identify the genetic basis of diseases (National Institute of Health, n.d.).

The completed database is a mosaic rather than any one individual. Its genetic and medicinal utility comes from the fact that over 99% of the human genome is the same in all humans. Among other findings, the project found more than 300,000 SNPs. The database provides benefits in many fields. It helps researchers understand diseases including viruses and mutations that cause different forms of cancer. The databases are open and available to everyone through the Internet.

For forensic science, the Human Genome Project has led to advancements in identification techniques. It was the groundwork for what is called next-generation sequencing (NGS). NGS technologies provide more sensitivity and speed than traditional STR sequencing and make it possible to analyze degraded samples and mixed DNA samples. It also provides the basis for investigative advancements such as genetic genealogy to solve cold cases. (Dewitt, 2024)

6.3.2 Combined DNA Index System

Unlike the Human Genome Project database, identification in criminal cases needs DNA profiles of individual humans. The FBI maintains such a database known as Combined DNA Index System (CODIS). CODIS describes the databases and the software used by the FBI for this purpose. The National DNA Index System (NDIS) is the part of CODIS containing the DNA profiles contributed by federal, state, and local laboratories.

The national DNA database was begun in 1998. It is now used to share DNA profiles across all 50 states, federal law enforcement agencies, and the Department of Defense. The CODIS software is also used by 58 countries for their own law enforcement identification purposes. The database now has over 20 million DNA profiles. CODIS links unknown DNA left during the commission of a crime to offenders and others who are legally required to provide samples for the database.

CODIS is designed to compare a DNA sample against the DNA records in the database. A match of the sample to a DNA profile in the database may be used as the basis for probable cause to get a court-ordered current DNA sample from the suspect. The local laboratory then performs a DNA analysis on the current suspect sample to be used as evidence in court.

CODIS primarily relies on STR profiling that analyzes short, repeated sequences of DNA. STR analysis has some limitations in its interpretation of degraded or mixed samples and the resolution of complex kinship relationships. The NGS produces more detailed DNA sequences that can identify not just STRs but also SNPs and other genetic markers. The FBI has not modified the CODIS software to use NGS but has facilitated federal government funding for local crime laboratories to implement NGS for routine casework.

6.4 THE ADMISSIBILITY OF DNA TESTIMONY

While the NAS Report was critical of the basis for some other types of forensic evidence, there is no remaining doubt about the reliability of most properly performed DNA analysis. The report found that "[a]mong existing forensic methods, only nuclear DNA analysis has been rigorously shown to have the capacity to consistently, and with a high degree of certainty, demonstrate a connection between an evidentiary sample and a specific individual or source." (National Research Council, 2009, at p. 100) DNA evidence is now universally admitted by courts in the United States because of its reliability and the fact that, absent fraud or an error in labeling or handling, the probabilities of a false positive are miniscule. The first use of DNA in a successful U.S. criminal prosecution was in *Andrews v. State*, 533 So.2d 841, 842 (Fla. Dist. Ct. App. 1988), when police matched DNA samples from semen to the defendant's blood in a rape case. The admission of DNA evidence in a criminal case was first approved by a state supreme court in *State v. Woodall*. 385 S.E.2d 253 (W. Va. 1989). Subsequently, properly collected and analyzed DNA evidence has been routinely admitted. DNA test results are now generally admissible in every U.S. jurisdiction. Many states have even adopted statutes authorizing admission of DNA evidence.

Other than issues of laboratory procedures and safeguards which present themselves in all forensic science cases, the admissibility questions concerning DNA which remain today arise mainly from the development and discovery of new methods of DNA analysis. Some forms of DNA evidence are now universally accepted as evidence of identity in U.S. courts as a matter of reliability.

Courts now universally accept the PCR process and the STR-based system of comparing alleles as reliable. It has reached the point where courts have held that there is no need to conduct a *Daubert* hearing or a *Frye* hearing since there is no disagreement in the scientific community about the reliability of those DNA processes. The use of random match probability (RMP) testimony to describe the statistical significance of a match between two PCR-STR single-source profiles has also been universally accepted.

The use of the paternal (Y-STR) and maternal DNA (mtDNA) analyses has been the subject of admissibility challenges in court. While the Y-STR process does not use the RMP analysis, most courts have accepted Y-STR typing results as reliable under *Frye* or *Daubert*. Admissibility challenges to mtDNA typing results, which also do not use the RMP analysis, have also been unsuccessful.

Improvements in DNA testing and interpretation methods mean that the quantity of DNA required for a profile is dramatically reduced. DNA profiles can be generated from a few skin cells. However, the admissibility of low copy number (LCN) DNA testing is still being contested. "Touch DNA," or more accurately "trace DNA," refers to the small amount of DNA that is transferred from a person to a person or object through direct physical contact. The DNA is usually swabbed from a surface or object. DNA samples involving a very small amount of DNA are more difficult to test and analyze. Several courts have nevertheless found LCN testing to be reliable, under both *Frye* and *Daubert*. But a few courts have excluded LCN testing results.

When crime scene samples contain a mixture of DNA from more than one person, it poses significant problems that may affect reliability. It can be difficult for analysts to determine which alleles at each locus belong to which person. RMP calculation using allelic frequencies is not possible in mixture situations. Some laboratories even adopt a policy of not interpreting highly complex mixtures.

> Distinguishing one person's DNA from another's in these mixtures, estimating how many individuals contributed DNA, determining whether the DNA is even relevant or is from contamination, or whether there is a trace amount of suspect or victim DNA makes DNA mixture interpretation inherently more challenging than examining single-source samples. These issues, if not properly considered and communicated, can lead to misunderstandings regarding the strength and relevance of the DNA evidence in a case.
>
> National Institute of Standards and Technology (2024)

New probabilistic genotyping software (PGS) programs may allow the calculation of mixture match statistics that can better enable separate identification. However, there are some *Daubert* issues that have yet to be resolved concerning PGS. There are a number of PGS software programs available, and their reliability may vary. The National Institute of Standards and Technology (NIST) Report says, "The degree of reliability or trustworthiness of a given PGS system in a given case is dependent upon the number of instances in which that system has been tested with samples that are judged to be of similar complexity as the casework sample, the performance of the method among those instances, and how the characteristics (e.g., number of contributors, DNA amounts, level of degradation) of the known samples compared to those of the sample in the case at hand." National Institute of Standards and Technology (2024 at p. 76). There are also issues about the lack of established standards for the various software programs, many of which are privately owned.

6.5 HUMAN ERROR

Although DNA profiling is clearly scientifically superior to other forensic identification evidence, it is not infallible. DNA evidence and its underlying methodology are, of course, subject to human error. False positive DNA results have occurred and will undoubtedly continue to be part of the DNA testing landscape. Proffered evidence may still, as with other forensic science evidence, be the result of mistakes or contamination in its collection, testing, or interpretation. As the technology and methodology of DNA testing has progressed, it is the human errors that may present the biggest evidentiary challenges for admissibility. DNA evidence has been recently challenged with a variety of factors, including poor laboratory proficiency testing, contamination, lack of proper laboratory protocols or accreditation, improper techniques, lack of quality control, and broken chains of custody. Laboratory temperature variances are a source of challenge because DNA is very sensitive to environmental conditions and can start to degrade depending on exposure to extreme temperatures or other factors. Before and at the laboratory, DNA testing errors can result from sample mislabeling, or otherwise switching samples, or from cross-contamination between samples in the same or different cases.

CASE STUDY Human Error?

PEOPLE V. GARY LEITERMAN

In 1969, Washtenaw County, Michigan, had witnessed a series of murders of young women in what became known as the "Michigan Murders." On March 19, 1969, Jane Mixer was a 23-year-old first-year law student at the University of Michigan. She had arranged to meet her boyfriend at her parent's home in Muskegon, Michigan, some two and a half hours away from the Ann Arbor law school, where they would announce their wedding plans. In what was a common practice at the time, she posted a note on a "ride board" in the basement of the law library seeking a ride to Muskegon. She told her boyfriend that a man who identified himself as "David Johnson" had responded to the posting and was going to pick her up at 6:00 p.m. on his way to Muskegon. On that evening, however, she called her boyfriend and said that Johnson had not appeared, and she was trying to contact him from her dorm room. At approximately 10:00 p.m., the roommate of a fellow student named David Johnson received a telephone call from a woman who identified herself as "Jane Mixer" and inquired whether Johnson still intended to drive her to Muskegon. The roommate told the caller that Johnson was on stage performing in a campus play at that moment and was not going to Muskegon that evening (Figure 6.4).

Jane Mixer never made it to Muskegon. The next day her body was found on top of a grave in a cemetery a few miles from Ann Arbor. She had been strangled with a stocking and shot twice in the head with a .22-caliber gun. Her pantyhose had been pulled down, but there was no evidence of a rape (Figure 6.5).

Figure 6.4 Jane Mixer.

Source: Washtenaw County Trial Court

Figure 6.5 Crime Scene Photo – Mixer Homicide.

Source: Washtenaw County Trial Court

The public assumed that it was another of the serial murders. Subsequently, a young man named John Norman Collins was arrested and convicted of one of the earlier murders and the killings stopped. Police were not so sure.

During the Mixer investigation, state police examined her dorm room and found a phonebook open to the page with listings for "David Johnson." Police determined that all of the David Johnsons associated with the university had alibis. During the investigation, one of the officers went to the area of the law library basement where the "ride board" was located. Because he also happened to be working on another case involving pay telephone fraud, he went into a pay telephone booth near the board. He saw a telephone book in the booth with the handwritten words "Mixer – Muskegon" on the cover. He collected the phone book as evidence. The investigation, however, went nowhere, and the police had no leads as to the killer. There was no DNA analysis available in 1969, and the Mixer case remained unsolved for 35 years.

In 2004, state police working in a "cold case" unit found the old box of evidence from the Mixer murder, including the victim's pantyhose. Some of the evidence was sent to the laboratory. On the pantyhose, the state police lab found five stains of a substance they believed was either sweat or saliva. DNA analysis from the lab was run through the CODIS DNA database, and it came back with a "hit." The DNA on Mixer's pantyhose matched a sample from a Gary Leiterman, a 62-year-old former nurse from the western side of Michigan who was in the national database because of a 2002 conviction for prescription fraud. The odds that the DNA on the stockings had come from someone other than Leiterman were 70 trillion to one (Figure 6.6).

The trial of Leiterman attracted the attention of the national media, and the trial was covered daily by the print media and by Court TV, which carried the entire trial live on its web site. CBS covered the case nationally and later aired a one-hour episode of "48 Hours Mystery" based on the case (CBS News, *Deadly Ride*, November 22, 2005).

Although the DNA evidence linking Leiterman to the killing was overwhelming, the prosecution had a significant problem. Photos of the Mixer's body at the cemetery showed a small drop of what appeared to be blood on her forearm. Police had scraped the small remnants of the blood into an evidence envelope. When the state police lab analyzed those remnants, they found DNA which they testified also found a match in the CODIS system – but not to Gary

Figure 6.6 Gary Leiterman.

Source: Washtenaw County Trial Court

Leiterman. According to the lab, the blood spot matched the DNA of a man named John Ruelas. In 2004, Ruelas was serving a life sentence in a Michigan prison for the murder of his mother, but Ruelas was only 4 years old at the time of the Mixer murder and was obviously not the murderer. It turned out that the police lab was examining Ruelas DNA in connection with his mother's murder at the same time they were analyzing the scraping from the blood spot on Jane Mixer's arm. Nevertheless, the laboratory steadfastly denied that it had contaminated the blood scraping with the Ruelas sample. The defense presented its own DNA expert who testified that he believed the samples had been cross contaminated (Figure 6.7).

There was other evidence against Leiterman, however. The phonebook found in the law library basement had been discarded but a photograph of the cover with the handwriting on it had been saved. A government handwriting expert compared the handwritten words "Mixer" and "Muskegon" with several 1969 samples of the defendant's

Figure 6.7 Blood Spot Analyzed as Ruelas DNA.

Source: Washtenaw County Trial Court

handwriting. He testified that it was "highly probable" that the defendant wrote the words on the phonebook cover. The defense offered a handwriting expert who testified that Leiterman's samples did not match the phone book writing.

Leiterman had lived and worked in the Ann Arbor area at the time of the killing. A former roommate testified that around that time he found a stack of newspapers kept by Leiterman on the floor of his bedroom closet. The newspapers the defendant saved all featured articles about John Norman Collins and the details of the serial "Michigan Murders." The roommate also testified that Leiterman owned a revolver and had even set up a firing range in the basement of their home. State records confirmed that in 1967, Leiterman had purchased and registered a six-shot .22-caliber Ruger revolver, which he later reported as having been stolen. During a December 2004 search of the defendant's house, however, the police seized a revolver cylinder that a state police firearms expert testified was "consistent with" the construction and design of such a Ruger pistol. A state police ballistics expert testified that bullet fragments removed from Mixer's brain were "similar" to several bullets found in the 2004 search and "could have been" fired from a .22-caliber six-shot Ruger revolver. The ballistics expert did admit, however, that there are more than three dozen models of guns capable of firing similar bullets.

Thirty witnesses testified during the two-week trial. Leiterman did not take the stand. The jury found him guilty of first-degree murder after deliberating for a few hours. The defendant hired a new lawyer and sought a new trial, but the trial judge refused.

On appeal to the Michigan Court of Appeals, Leiterman claimed that the evidence of contamination was so strong that the DNA evidence was inadmissible under the *Daubert* standards used in Michigan. The defense offered the affidavit of a new DNA expert, a Dr. Kessis, who again asserted that the contamination of the blood spot scrapings made DNA evidence from the pantyhose stains unreliable. The appellate court disagreed:

> We need not, however, address the merits of Kessis' challenges to the testing conducted by the state police crime lab as to the reliability and, therefore, its admissibility. Indeed, the Court in Daubert specifically counseled courts to respect the differing functions of judge and jury-stating that the focus of the reliability inquiry "must be upon the principles and methodology, not on the conclusions that they generate." . . . Thus, we join those courts that have concluded that because challenges such as those raised by Kessis concern the manner in which a method is applied in a particular case rather than the validity of the method, they affect the weight that should be given to the evidence rather than its admissibility.
>
> Because the type of testing employed in this case has received general acceptance as reliable, . . . any objection to its results are relevant to the weight of the testimony and not its admissibility. Indeed, the alleged errors identified by Kessis, and relied on by defendant in seeking a new trial in this matter, are insufficient to skew the otherwise reliable PCR methodology used in this case. Rather, the alleged errors strike at the weight of the evidence introduced by the prosecution. There was, therefore, no error in the admission of the testimony at trial, and the trial court did not abuse its discretion in denying defendant's motion for a new trial on that ground. People v. Gary Lieterman (2007) at p. 5–6

The Court also rejected Leiterman's claim that his retained trial attorney had been ineffective to the extent that a new trial was required. The conviction was affirmed. Leiterman's application for leave to appeal to the Michigan Supreme Court was denied on January 8, 2008. His subsequent federal appeals were also denied. He died in prison in 2019.

CASE STUDY Whose DNA Gets Put Into CODIS?

CODIS is the FBI software used to create a database of DNA profiles for use by law enforcement to compare crime scene DNA samples to samples of persons whose DNA profiles have previously been entered in the database. While there are samples in the database from federal law enforcement and other federal sources, many of the profiles in CODIS are submitted by State and local law enforcement agencies. Whether a person is forced to have their DNA sampled through a buccal swab is left to the laws of each State. Originally States mandated DNA sampling from prisoners, then some expanded it to persons convicted of violent crimes, and then to persons convicted of felonies, and then to persons convicted of misdemeanor crimes. Finally, some States required or allowed DNA sampling of any person arrested for a violent crime, regardless of whether any charges were ever filed. In 2013, the Maryland law allowing forced DNA sampling from some arrestees was challenged in the U.S. Supreme Court.

> In 2009 Alonzo King was arrested in Wicomico County, Maryland, and charged with first- and second-degree assault for menacing a group of people with a shotgun. As part of a routine [Maryland] booking procedure for serious offenses, his DNA sample was taken by applying a cotton swab or filter paper – known as a buccal swab – to the inside of his cheeks. Maryland v. King (2013) at p. 440

King's DNA was analyzed and entered in the CODIS, and it was found to match DNA taken from a 2003 rape victim. King was subsequently convicted of the rape. He appealed his conviction on Fourth Amendment grounds that there was no probable cause and no warrant for taking his DNA sample when he was arrested for the assault charge.

The Maryland law authorized Maryland police to collect DNA samples from "an individual who is charged with . . . a crime of violence or an attempt to commit a crime of violence; or . . . burglary or an attempt to commit burglary." The Supreme Court, in a 5–4 opinion, first reviewed the STR profiling process as producing a "near certainty" of identification. The majority then described the buccal swab process as

> a far more gentle process than a venipuncture to draw blood. It involves but a light touch on the inside of the cheek; and although it can be deemed a search within the body of the arrestee, it requires no "surgical intrusions beneath the skin." . . . The fact that an intrusion is negligible is of central relevance to determining reasonableness, although it is still a search as the law defines that term. Maryland v. King (2013) at p. 448

The majority of the Court denied King's appeal on the ground that taking a DNA sample is simply part of the "routine booking process," just like taking fingerprints, in order to identify the person under arrest:

> In light of the context of a valid arrest supported by probable cause respondent's expectations of privacy were not offended by the minor intrusion of a brief swab of his cheeks. By contrast, that same context of arrest gives rise to significant state interests in identifying respondent not only so that the proper name can be attached to his charges but also so that the criminal justice system can make informed decisions concerning pretrial custody. Upon these considerations the Court concludes that DNA identification of arrestees is a reasonable search that can be considered part of a routine booking procedure. When officers make an arrest supported by probable cause to hold for a serious offense and they bring the suspect to the station to be detained in custody, taking and analyzing a cheek swab of the arrestee's DNA is, like fingerprinting and photographing, a legitimate police booking procedure that is reasonable under the Fourth Amendment. Maryland v. King (2013) at p. 465–466

Four justices dissented, including Justice Scalia who wrote:

> It is obvious that no such noninvestigative motive exists in this case. The Court's assertion that DNA is being taken, not to solve crimes, but to *identify* those in the State's custody, taxes the credulity of the credulous. And the Court's comparison of Maryland's DNA searches to other techniques, such as fingerprinting, can seem apt only to those who know no more than today's opinion has chosen to tell them about how those DNA searches actually work. Maryland v. King (2013) at p. 466

WHAT DO YOU THINK?

The *King* case meant that States could mandate taking DNA samples from persons who were arrested but not convicted and that DNA could be entered in CODIS and used to convict the arrestee of a crime other than what the person was arrested for. Is allowing the police to take a DNA sample no more personally intrusive than fingerprinting? What other than identity does a fingerprint disclose? On the other hand, can a DNA sample disclose virtually everything about a person's makeup? The majority pointed out that the STR analysis used in CODIS "does not show more far-reaching and complex characteristics like genetic traits." But what about the existence of the sample itself? Can you think of anyone who might be interested in getting ahold of all the genetic and medical information about individuals? Maybe insurance companies, for example?

REFERENCES

Andrews v. State, 533 So.2d 841, 842 (Fla. Dist. Ct. App. 1988)

CBS News, *Deadly Ride* (November 22, 2005) https://www.cbsnews.com/news/deadly-ride/

Dewitt, J., *Beginner's Guide to Next Generation Sequencing*, Integrated Data Technologies (May 15, 2024) https://www.idtdna.com/page/support-and-education/decoded-plus/what-is-next-generation-sequencing

Maryland v. King, 569 U.S. 435 (2013)

National Institute of Health, *The Human Genome Project*, https://www.genome.gov/human-genome-project

National Institute of Justice, *What is STR Analysis?* (March 2, 2011) https://nij.ojp.gov/topics/articles/what-str-analysis

National Institute of Science and Technology, *DNA Mixture Interpretation: A NIST Scientific Foundation Review* (2024) https://www.nist.gov/spo/forensic-science-program/dna-mixture-interpretation-nist-scientific-foundation-review#

National Research Council of the National Academies of Science, *Strengthening Forensic Science in the United States: A Path Forward* (2009), p. 185. https://nap.nationalacademies.org/catalog/12589/strengthening-forensic-science-in-the-united-states-a-path-forward

Pedroza, S. and Iyavoo, S., *Implementation of NGS and SNP Microarrays in Routine Forensic Practice: Opportunities and Barriers*, 26 BMC Genomics 541 (2025) https://doi.org/10.1186/s12864-025-11723-6

People v. Gary Lieterman, Mich. Ct. App. (July 24, 2007) https://law.justia.com/cases/michigan/court-of-appeals-unpublished/2007/20070724-c265821-79-265821-opn.html

State v. Woodall. 385 S.E.2d 253 (W. Va. 1989)

U.S. Department of Justice, *Advancing Justice Through DNA Technology: Using DNA to Solve Crimes*, https://www.justice.gov/archives/ag/advancing-justice-through-dna-technology-using-dna-solve-crimes

READINGS

Bukyya, J., et al., *DNA Profiling in Forensic Science: A Review*, 8(4) Glob. Med. Genet. 31 (2021) https://pmc.ncbi.nlm.nih.gov/articles/PMC8635824/

Butler, J., et al., *DNA Mixture Interpretation: A NIST Scientific Foundation Review*, National Institute of Standards and Technology (2024) https://doi.org/10.6028/NIST.IR.8351

Federal Bureau of Investigation, *Booking Station Rapid DNA and Combined DNA Index System (CODIS)* https://le.fbi.gov/science-and-lab/biometrics-and-fingerprints/codis/rapid-dna

Federal Bureau of Investigation, *The FBI's Combined DNA Index System (CODIS) Hits Major Milestone* (May 21, 2021) https://www.fbi.gov/news/press-releases/the-fbis-combined-dna-index-system-codis-hits-major-milestone

Federal Bureau of Investigation, *Frequently Asked Questions on CODIS and NDIS*, https://www.fbi.gov/how-we-can-help-you/dna-fingerprint-act-of-2005-expungement-policy/codis-and-ndis-fact-sheet

Genome Link, *Open-Source DNA Databases: What They Are and How to Use Them* (February 11, 2023) https://genomelink.io/blog/open-source-dna-databases

Kaye, D., *Why So Contrived? Fourth Amendment Balancing, Per Se Rules, and DNA Databases After Maryland v. King*, 104 J. Crim. L. Criminology 535 (2014). https://scholarlycommons.law.northwestern.edu/jclc/vol104/iss3/2

Khehra, N., Padda, I. and Zubair M., *Polymerase Chain Reaction (PCR)* (2025) https://www.ncbi.nlm.nih.gov/books/NBK589663/

Mallios, C., *Supreme Court Upholds DNA Collection of Arrestees*, U.S. Department of Justice (June 2013) https://www.ojp.gov/ncjrs/virtual-library/abstracts/supreme-court-upholds-dna-collection-arrestees

Miko, I., *Gregor Mendel and the Principles of Inheritance*, 1(1) Nat. Educ. 134 (2008) https://www.nature.com/scitable/topicpage/gregor-mendel-and-the-principles-of-inheritance-593/

Pray, L., *Discovery of DNA Structure and Function: Watson and Crick*, 1(1) Nat. Educ. 100 (2008) https://www.nature.com/scitable/topicpage/discovery-of-dna-structure-and-function-watson-397/

University of Leicester, *DNA Fingerprinting*, https://le.ac.uk/dna-fingerprinting

University of Utah, *Making SNPs Make Sense*, https://learn.genetics.utah.edu/content/precision/snips/

7

Hair Comparison

Hair analysis can be a forensic tool because human hairs are routinely shed and can easily be discovered at a crime scene. Examination of hair found at the scene and compared with hair from a known source may be helpful to the extent that it reflects similarities. The extent of the similarity in those samples and the examiner's ability to discover and compare those similarities is the principal issue when hair analysis is offered in a criminal case. Microscopic hair examination and analysis have been undertaken for over a century, but it has been discovered that they have a very limited capability to identify individuals. Recent developments in DNA testing have greatly expanded the ability of hair sample examination to make individual identifications.

7.1 MICROSCOPIC HAIR ANALYSIS

Traditionally, forensic evidence comparing human hair was based on a microscopic comparison of the evidentiary sample with a known sample from the defendant. To make a microscopic hair comparison, a control group of hairs from a known source must be properly collected by pulling or combing hairs from a subject. That requires a total of 50 hairs from different areas of the scalp or a total of 25 hairs from a pubic region. The samples are then examined macroscopically for gross feature comparison, such as color, form, and thickness. In the microscopic stage, hairs are mounted on slides using a mounting medium that has the same refractive index as the hair. The hair analyst then attempts to identify the part of the body from which the hair might have come, based on certain area characteristics.

DOI: 10.4324/9781041136361-9

The features of the hair are divided into major and secondary characteristics. Major characteristics include color, treatment, pigment aggregation, shaft form, pigment distribution, medulla appearance, hair diameter, medullary index, and the presence or absence of a root or shaft. Secondary characteristics include cuticular margin, pigment density, pigment size, tip shape, and shaft diameter. The examiner then formulates an opinion as to exclusion or consistency.

Although previously used by investigative agencies, including the FBI, it is now uniformly recognized that microscopic hair comparisons do not constitute a basis for a definitive identification. DNA discovered that microscopic hair comparison led to three wrongful convictions and exonerations (Cole, 2023). The FBI then undertook a review of a sample of the over 21,000 cases in which its experts had testified based on hair microscopy.

After reversal of a few convictions, the FBI began a review of available court transcripts and reports in 2012. Their review of Microscopic Hair Comparison Analysis (MHCA) found report and testimony errors . . . that occurred for decades prior to 2000. These report and testimony errors occurred when examiners made statements beyond what the science of this discipline would support, such as stating the hair found at a crime scene came from a known source (e.g. suspect or victim). In 2015, the FBI publicly announced the interim findings of their internal review, which found errors in most of the reports and transcripts reviewed.

FBI, Root Cause Analysis of Microscopic Hair Analysis (2018)

Claims by a prosecutor or an expert of a "match" based on hair analysis are gross overstatements of the capabilities of microscopic hair analysis. The NAS Report assessed the state of microscopic hair analysis:

> No scientifically accepted statistics exist about the frequency with which particular characteristics of hair are distributed in the population. There appear to be no uniform standards on the number of features on which hairs must agree before an examiner may declare a "match." . . . The committee found no scientific support for the use of hair comparisons for individualization in the absence of nuclear DNA.
>
> National Research Council (2009) at p. 156

7.2 DNA ANALYSIS OF HAIR SAMPLES

The advent of DNA, and particularly the mtDNA method, changed the field of forensic hair analysis. More recent developments have taken the science a step further. The strands of hair from a crime scene are often only the shaft of the hair that has broken or fallen from the root, which remains in the body. If the evidence sample has a root, typical and much more definitive nuclear DNA can be used. In that case, it becomes like any other DNA examination and the hair is simply the place where the DNA was found.

If the shaft does not have a root, scientists first discovered that the shaft still contained some mitochondrial mtDNA. The mtDNA analysis is not as discriminating as nuclear DNA, since it is based on mitochondria in human cells, which are shared by maternal relatives. Thus, siblings will be indistinguishable based on mtDNA comparison. In spite of that limitation, the value of mtDNA comparison was that mitochondria are found outside the nuclei of human cells and exist in shafts of hair that have no roots

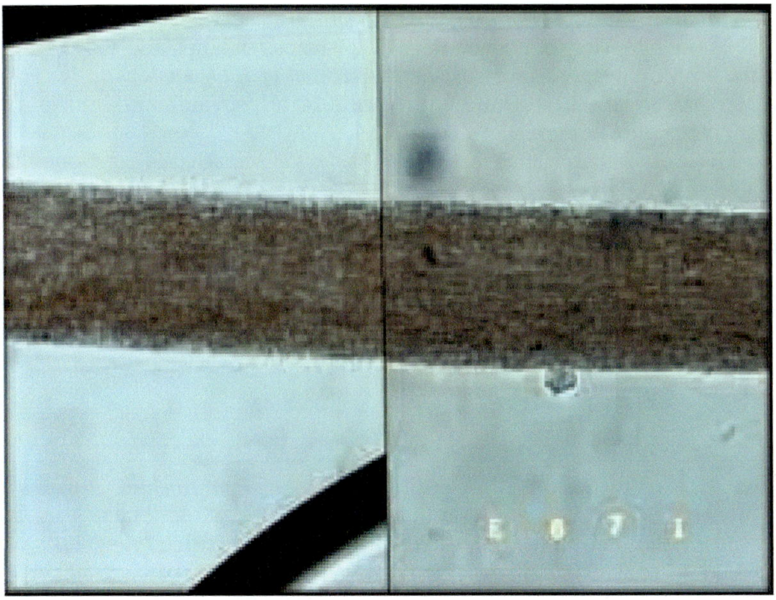

Figure 7.1 Microscopic Hair Comparison.

Source: University of Colorado Boulder

attached. Where there is no root, as is often the case, mtDNA could effectively be used to supplant, or at least support, a microscopic hair analysis. With the limitations on the accuracy of microscopic comparisons, mtDNA analysis could give the court a more substantial basis for admitting hair analysis as a significant part of a prosecution.

More recently, developments in DNA extraction and analysis may change the field even further. Scientists have now discovered that there is indeed identifiable nuclear DNA in the strands of hair even without a root (Fatima, 2024). There are proprietary programs that have been able to extract enough DNA from a hair strand to formulate a profile. If these developments meet the *Daubert* criteria, particularly with regard to error rate, this would mean that a hair, including a strand without a root, is simply another location where DNA can be found, examined, and compared (Figure 7.1).

REFERENCES

Cole, S., et al., *Microscopic Hair Analysis Comparison and Convicting the Innocent*, The National Registry of Exonerations (2023) https://n2t.net/ark:/88112/x2d909

Fatima, T., Munawar, A. and Yaseen, J., *Potential of Hair Analysis in the Field of Forensic Science*, 2(1) FIHSB 23–18 (April 2024) https://ammanif.com/journal/fi/index.php/home/article/view/131

Federal Bureau of Investigation, *Root Cause Analysis of Microscopic Hair Analysis* (2018) https://vault.fbi.gov/root-cause-analysis-of-microscopic-hair-comparison-analysis/

National Research Council of the National Academies of Science, *Analysis of Hair Evidence*, Strengthening Forensic Science in the United States: A Path Forward (2009) https://nap.nationalacademies.org/catalog/12589/strengthening-forensic-science-in-the-united-states-a-path-forward

READINGS

Fatima, T., Munawar, A. and Yaseen, J., *Potential of Hair Analysis in the Field of Forensic Science*, 2(1) Forensic Insights Health Sci. Bull. 23–18 (April 2024) https://ammanif.com/journal/fi/index.php/home/article/view/131

Grisedale, K., et al., *Successful Nuclear DNA Profiling of Rootless Hair Shafts: A Novel Approach*, 132(1) Int. J. Legal Med. 107–115 (2017/January 2018) https://pubmed.ncbi.nlm.nih.gov/28993934/

Liu, Z., et al., *DNA and Protein Analyses of Hair in Forensic Genetics*, 137(3) Int. J. Legal Med. 613–633 (May 2023) https://pubmed.ncbi.nlm.nih.gov/36732435/

Norton, J., Anderson, W. and Divine, G., *Flawed Forensics: Statistical Failings of Microscopic Hair Analysis*, Royal Statistical Society (2016) https://doi.org/10.1111/j.1740-9713.2016.00897.x

Puri, A. and Arya, N., *Hair Analysis*, chapter in *Fundamentals of Forensic Biology*, Puri, A., Mahalakshmi, N., Chauhan, T., Mishra, A. and Bhatnagar, P. (Eds.) (2024). Springer. https://doi.org/10.1007/978-981-99-3161-3_33

Smith, S. and Linch, C., *A Review of Major Factors Contributing to Errors in Human Hair Association by Microscopy*, 20(3) Am. J. Forensic Med. Pathol. 269–273 (September 1999) https://pubmed.ncbi.nlm.nih.gov/10507796/

8

Fingerprints

Friction Ridge Analysis

8.1 THE FINGERPRINT DEVELOPMENT AND STORAGE PROCESS

Analysis of the images left by prints from the fingers, palms, or soles is more properly known as friction ridge analysis. Simply put, it is an examiner's comparison of impressions left by ridges on the skin in two samples. It has traditionally been used to make an identification of a person, such as during an arrest or death investigation, or to prove than an individual touched a surface where one of the ridge impressions was left. Early work was by a simple visual analysis of patent, or obvious, prints left at the scene of a crime.

Skin is never completely dry or clean. Dirt or oil, or even sweat, leaves impressions whenever a solid surface is touched. Fingerprints are reproduced images of the ridged surfaces on the skin that result when oil is transferred from the skin onto the surface of the area which was touched. If the hands are stained, or if the surface is soft, the print may be visible to the naked eye and is known as patent fingerprint. Most fingerprints are not visible without being enhanced in some way and are known as latent fingerprints. The quality of impression evidence and its eventual analysis depend a great deal on the procedures used to collect, preserve, and enhance the evidence discovered at the scene. Forensic scientists can visualize them through a variety of enhancement means, originally called "dusting," but we now have a whole range of techniques for finding and enhancing print images.

DOI: 10.4324/9781041136361-10

There are generally three types of techniques for making latent fingerprints visible: physical, chemical, and instrumental. The basic physical process for visualizing fingerprints at a scene is "dusting" the suspected area with a powder that then adheres to the oils or other matter left by the ridges. This process is most effective on smooth surfaces that do not absorb the oils. The prints revealed by the dusting can be photographed directly. More often the prints are "lifted" from the surface using tape and that taped image is then pressed onto and transferred to a printed card (Figure 8.1).

A common chemical technique is called "cyanoacrylate fuming," or more colloquially "super glue fuming." Fingerprints leave traces of amino acids, fatty acids, and proteins which will react to the fumes produced when superglue is heated. That reaction forms a sticky, white material that clings to the ridges of fingerprints, making them visible. Items to be tested are placed inside an airtight chamber, a few drops of "super glue" are placed into a heating tray inside the chamber, and the reaction leaves white outlines of the ridges which can then be photographed directly or dusted, lifted, and transferred. This chemical process is especially effective on textures or other surfaces that are not very susceptible to physical visualization. The reaction is not permanent so the print must be photographed or transferred soon after development.

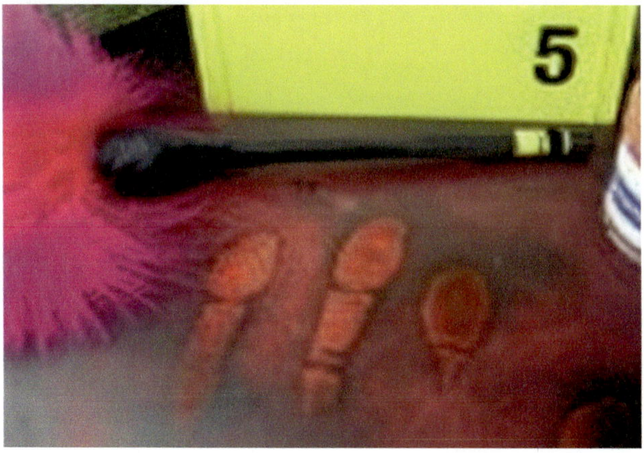

Figure 8.1 Fingerprint Dusting.

Source: http://www.indianapolisdocumentexaminer.com/

Other chemicals also react with the chemical in the fingerprint residue and the most common chemical technique for porous surfaces today involves ninhydrin. The chemical reaction of the ninhydrin with the oils from the hand reveals prints in a high-contrast purple tone. Ninhydrin development occurs slowly at room temperature and normal humidity. Various treatments are then used to enhance the prints, including treatment with metal-based reagents to intensify the prints (Figures 8.2 and 8.3).

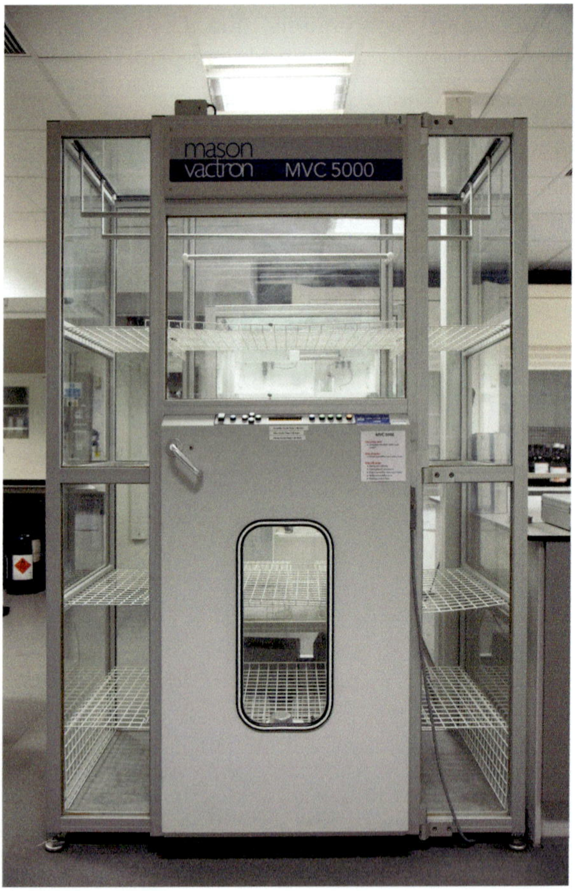

Figure 8.2 Fuming Tank.

Source: Fisher Scientific

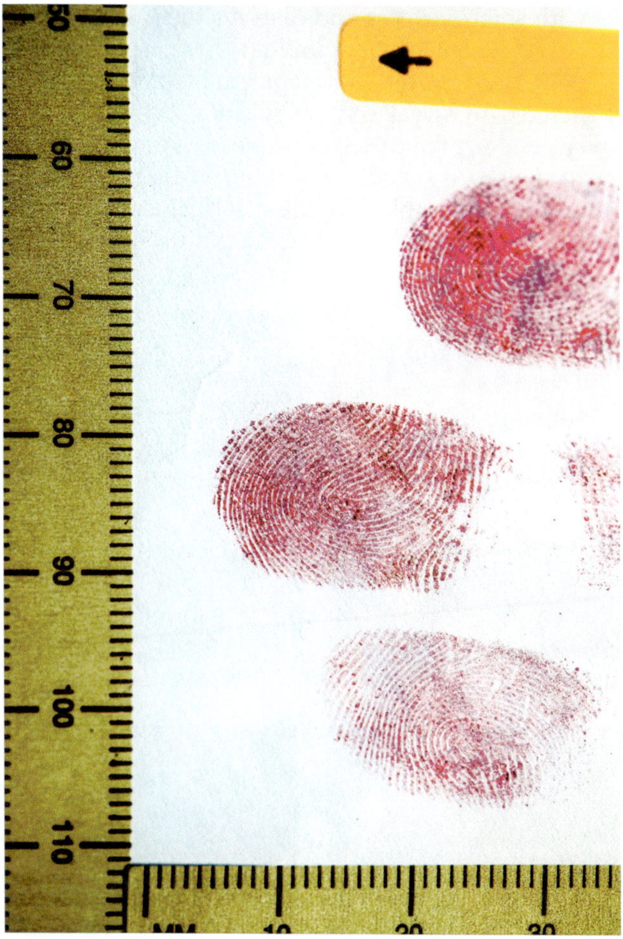

Figure 8.3 Ninhydrin.

Source: Kevin Malahy, Pinterest

Instrumental techniques have been developed and tested and each may be more appropriate in a given case depending on the conditions and the materials. One development of an instrumental technique for fingerprint detection involves the use of a scanning Kelvin microprobe. The device maps the changes in electrical impulses left when the skin comes into contact with some surfaces and displays the electrochemical images of the patterns of that contact. It requires no physical or chemical change in the suspected surface. Another development is Micro-X-ray fluorescence. Body salts excreted in sweat contain sodium, potassium, and chlorine that are deposited along the patterns present in a fingerprint. An image of the fingerprint can be visualized by shining a thin beam of X-rays onto it without disturbing the sample. The chemical elements emit radiation at a "signature" frequency revealed in a spectrograph (Figure 8.4).

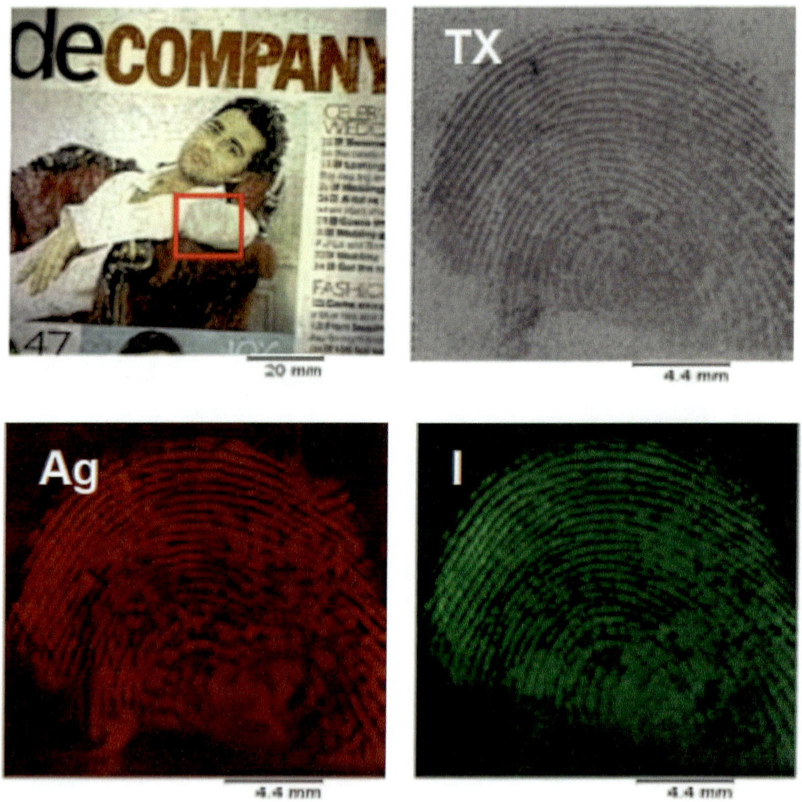

Figure 8.4 Micro X-Ray Fingerprint.

Source: Horiba Scientific https://www.horiba.com/esp/scientific/applications/others/pages/fingerprint-imaging-with-micro-xrf/

The other part of the fingerprinting process involves imaging and recording fingerprints of a known individual for later comparison. Inked fingerprint cards were long accepted as the standard means for recording and storing fingerprint data and evolved into an accepted international standard for the exchange of fingerprint identification between criminal justice agencies. The FBI developed detailed specifications for taking fingerprints that were used by virtually all police agencies in the United States. The impressions were recorded on a standard fingerprint identification card. The upper ten impressions are taken individually of the thumb, index, middle, ring, and little fingers of each hand. These were referred to as the "rolled" impressions because the fingers are rolled from one side of the fingernail to the other, in order to obtain all available ridge detail.

Today the FBI and most local agencies use an inkless digital system for recording fingerprints called Livescan. Fingerprints are scanned to produce digital images which can be electronically transmitted to the FBI and or other investigating agencies. The technology replaces the ink rolling process and can avoid common problems with ink fingerprints such as smudging, smearing, and using too much or too little ink. The FBI has developed complex standards for digital scanning devices (Figure 8.5).

Digital devices are not without their own problems. Different types of digital scanners are available. The scanners measure the difference between the ridges and valleys using various elements such as optical or thermal differences. However, when a finger touches or rolls onto a surface, the skin may deform based on the pressure applied by the user or by various skin conditions. There is also concern that the projection of an irregular three-dimensional finger onto a two-dimensional scanner may introduce distortion. Non-contact three-dimensional fingerprint scanners have been developed that compensate for many of these problems.

The national fingerprint identification software and database was originally called the Automated Fingerprint Identification System (AFIS). It was essentially a searchable database based on fingerprints submitted by federal, state, and local agencies. In 2011, the FBI replaced AFIS with what is called the Next Generation Identification (NGI) system, which included what is now called Advanced Fingerprint Identification Technology (AFIT). According to the FBI, the AFIT has enhanced fingerprint and latent processing services, increased the accuracy and daily

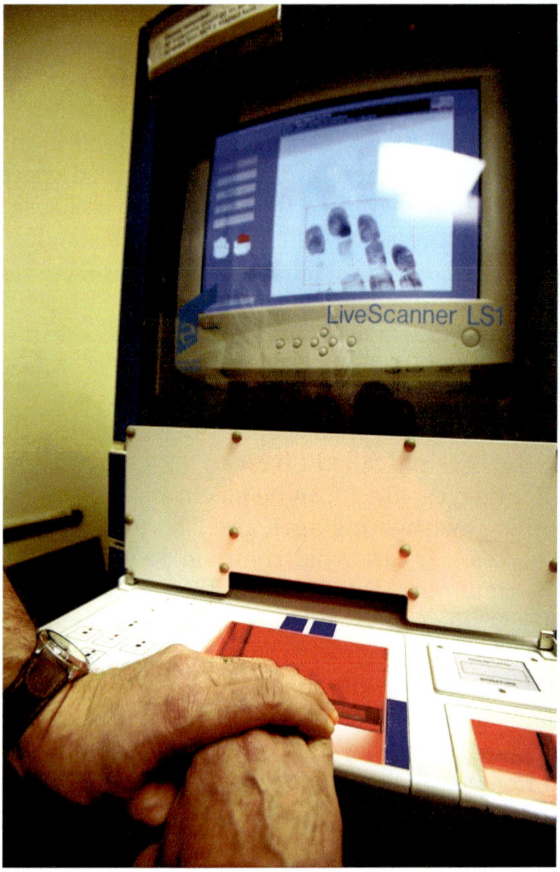

Figure 8.5 Livescan.

Source: Mission Peak Scouts https://missionpeakscouts.com/use-this-form-for-livescan-fingerprints/

fingerprint processing capacity, and improved system availability. It claims that a new fingerprint-matching algorithm has matching accuracy of more than 99.6%. The NGI has fingerprints and criminal histories of over 185 million people (Federal Bureau of Investigation, Next Generation Identification, n.d.).

8.2 FINGERPRINT COMPARISON

The forensic science community has long regarded friction ridge analysis as a primary method for assessing "individualization," the conclusion that a suspect fingerprint impression comes, unambiguously, from a single person. Searching the NGI database is a comparison of known images of fingerprints which may be of differing qualities with a crime scene fingerprint image, which may be partial and of more questionable clarity. The database search may return several possibilities. Ultimately the comparison of known and questioned fingerprints is done by a human fingerprint examiner. The established technique used to examine fingerprints goes by the acronym ACE-V, for "Analysis, Comparison, Evaluation, and Verification."

The analysis phase of an unknown print requires the examiner to consider the many factors that may affect the detail in the latent print, including the condition of the skin (aging, damage to the skin scars, diseases, and masking attempts), the type and amount of residue (sweat, oil, blood, paint, etc.), the mechanics of the touch (pressure on the surface of the skin, flexibility of the ridges, furrows, and creases, etc.), the surface which was touched (texture, rigidity, shape, condition, and background), the development technique, the capture technique (photograph or lifting material), and the percentage of the surface available for comparison. The examiner also analyzes the known prints for factors that can affect its quality. If either print does not have sufficient detail for either identification or exclusion, the prints are considered "of no value" or "not suitable" for comparison.

The comparison phase consists of visually measuring and comparing the corresponding details in the suspect print and a known print. The observations might include "the overall shape of the latent print, anatomical aspects, ridge flows, ridge counts, shape of the core, delta location and shape, lengths of the ridges, minutia location and type, thickness of the ridges and furrows, shapes of the ridges, pore position, crease patterns and shapes, scar shapes, and temporary feature shapes."

The evaluation phase requires the examiner to consider the extent of the agreement of the ridge formations in the two prints and the sufficiency of the detail present to establish an identification called a "source determination." A "source determination" is made when the examiner concludes that there is sufficient quantity and quality of detail in agreement between the latent print and the known print. A "source exclusion" is made when there is disagreement between the latent and known prints.

If the detail is insufficient for either, it is deemed an "inconclusive comparison." The evaluation phase is the crucial comparison of similarities between the known and questioned prints. Those similarities are based on three basic patterns of fingerprint ridges, known as arch, loop, and whorl (Figures 8.6 and 8.7).

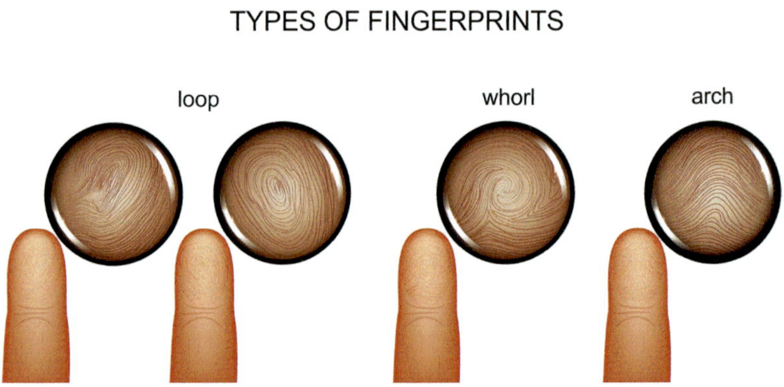

Figure 8.6 Types of Fingerprints.

Source: Susan DeForge

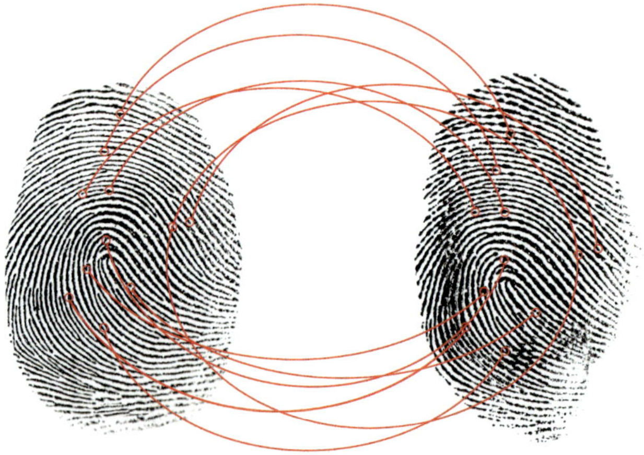

Figure 8.7 Fingerprint Comparison.

Source: iStock

The examiner then attempts to find these same basic types in the known and questioned prints.

The verification phase requires that another qualified examiner repeat the observations and come to the same conclusion. However, it is not a "blind" comparison since the standard practice allows the second examiner to be aware of the conclusion of the first examiner.

Despite the seeming formality of the fingerprint analysis process adopted by qualified examiners, the reality is that the assessment of fingerprint identification is nevertheless a subjective human interpretation. As the National Academies Report stated:

> Although some Automated Fingerprint Identification Systems (AFIS) permit fully automated identification of fingerprint records related to criminal history (e.g., for screening job applicants), the assessment of latent prints from crime scenes is based largely on human interpretation. Note that the ACE-V method does not specify particular measurements or a standard test protocol, and examiners must make subjective assessments throughout. In the United States, the threshold for making a source identification is deliberately kept subjective, so that the examiner can take into account both the quantity and quality of comparable details. As a result, the outcome of a friction ridge analysis is not necessarily repeatable from examiner to examiner.
>
> This subjectivity is intrinsic to friction ridge analysis, as can be seen when comparing it with DNA analysis. . . . For these reasons, population statistics for fingerprints have not been developed, and friction ridge analysis relies on subjective judgments by the examiner. Little research has been directed toward developing population statistics, although more would be feasible.
>
> National Research Council (2009) at p. 139

Fingerprint examiners regard their expertise as a matter of qualitative rather than quantitative analysis. They claim that the ability to see details in prints and the ability to compare features in prints is an "acquired skill" gained through experience and a lengthy apprenticeship. They deny that it is possible to establish numerical scores or thresholds based on corresponding features because they do not determine which features are relevant until they make their initial analysis and comparison.

Fingerprint examiners report a positive identification when they conclude that two different persons could not have produced the latent print. This is a subjective assessment. While examiners would be more accurate to use statistics to assign match probabilities based on population distributions of certain friction ridge features, most examiners generally refuse to do so. They claim that published statistical models only count corresponding minutiae and do not incorporate elements of clarity.

8.3 FINGERPRINT TESTIMONY UNDER DAUBERT AND FRYE ANALYSIS

The challenge of *Daubert* should be significant if it is applied to fingerprinting. On the one hand, most if not all of the claims made by or on behalf of fingerprint examiners enjoy unquestioning belief among the lay public, as well as judges and lawyers. On the other hand, fingerprint analysis may not meet much of the *Daubert* test for reliability. The first *Daubert* criterion is whether the method has been tested and, if so, what its error rate is. Many of the most basic tenets of fingerprint identification have never been subjected to empirical analysis. Proficiency testing that has been conducted does not support the zero error rate claimed by fingerprint examiners. An important *Daubert* criterion is whether there are established standards within the method. Crucially, while examiners debate about the number of points of similarity in fingerprints that are sufficient to declare a match, there is no generally accepted scientific or court-recognized minimum standard. Most modern researchers who have examined fingerprinting comparison have concluded that the broad claims of fingerprint identification accuracy cannot be substantiated under a *Daubert* analysis for reliability (Benedict, 2004).

The summary assessment of fingerprint analysis in the National Academies Report was somewhat less critical but did cast doubt on the ready acceptance of fingerprint expert testimony:

> Historically, friction ridge analysis has served as a valuable tool, both to identify the guilty and to exclude the innocent. Because of the amount of detail available in friction ridges, it seems plausible that a careful comparison of two impressions can accurately discern whether or not they had a common source. Although there is limited information about the accuracy and reliability of friction ridge analyses, claims that these analyses have zero error rates are not scientifically plausible.
>
> ACE-V provides a broadly stated framework for conducting friction ridge analyses. However, this framework is not specific enough to qualify as a validated method for this type of analysis. ACE-V does not guard against bias; is too broad to ensure repeatability and transparency; and

> does not guarantee that two analysts following it will obtain the same results. For these reasons, merely following the steps of ACE-V does not imply that one is proceeding in a scientific manner or producing reliable results. . . . Error rate is a much more difficult challenge. Errors can occur with any judgment-based method, especially when the factors that lead to the ultimate judgment are not documented. Some in the latent print community argue that the method itself, if followed correctly (i.e., by well-trained examiners properly using the method), has a zero error rate. Clearly, this assertion is unrealistic, and, moreover, it does not lead to a process of method improvement. . . . Some scientific evidence supports the presumption that friction ridge patterns are unique to each person and persist unchanged throughout a lifetime. Uniqueness and persistence are necessary conditions for friction ridge identification to be feasible, but those conditions do not imply that anyone can reliably discern whether or not two friction ridge impressions were made by the same person. Uniqueness does not guarantee that prints from two different people are always sufficiently different that they cannot be confused, or that two impressions made by the same finger will also be sufficiently similar to be discerned as coming from the same source.
>
> National Research Council (2009) at pp. 142–144

Given the general lack of validity testing for fingerprinting; the relative dearth of difficult proficiency tests; the lack of a statistically valid model of fingerprinting; and the lack of validated standards for declaring a match, such claims of absolute, certain confidence in identification are unjustified. . . . Therefore, in order to pass scrutiny under *Daubert*, fingerprint identification experts should exhibit a greater degree of epistemological humility. Claims of "absolute" and "positive" identification should be replaced by more modest claims about the meaning and significance of a "match."

Mnookin, Jennifer, *The Validity of Latent Fingerprint Identification: Confessions of a Fingerprinting Moderate*, 7 Law, Probability and Risk 111 (2008).

While *Daubert* should clearly be a more difficult admissibility test for fingerprinting, that has not been the case. The decisions of many courts exemplify the resistance of courts to any challenge to the admissibility of fingerprint testimony. Some have even held that trial judges are not even required to hold a *Daubert* or *Frye* hearing on a fingerprint challenge absent "novel" issues. And most courts that have re-examined fingerprint identification under *Daubert* have either held that it passed *Daubert* muster or have just continued to give it a superficial review and approval [U.S. v. Abreu, 406 F.3d 1304 (11th Cir. 2005); U.S. v. Havvard, 260 F.3d 597 (7th Cir. 2001)].

On the other hand, it seems logical that States that still use the *Frye* analysis will have little difficulty with fingerprinting testimony because fingerprint identification is certainly "generally accepted" and has been for a long time. Most of the claims made by fingerprint examiners enjoy widespread belief among members of both the public and the bar. In a sense, this points out the significant limitation of the *Frye* test, in that the criminal justice systems using that test take a very long time to react to changes in science, which often can take place in a short period of time. Fingerprinting might nevertheless face some challenges in *Frye* states. At least one Frye state judge found it to be "a subjective, untested, unverifiable identification procedure."

> The State is correct that fingerprint evidence has been used in criminal cases for almost a century. While that fact is worthy of consideration, it does not prove reliability. For many centuries, perhaps for millennia, humans thought that the earth was flat. The idea has a certain intuitive appeal. Indeed, there still exists a Flat Earth Society for people who cling to the idea the earth is not an orb. But science has proved that the earth is not flat; and, it is the type of fact of which a court can take judicial notice.
>
> *State v. Rose*, Case No. K06-0545 (Md. Balt. Co. Cir. Oct. 19, 2007), http://www.baltimoresun.com/media/acrobat/2007-10/33446162.pdf.

CASE STUDY The Brandon Mayfield Case

On March 11, 2004, terrorists blew up several trains in Madrid Spain, killing over 200 people and injuring another 1,400 people. Spanish police found a bag containing explosive detonators and retrieved a

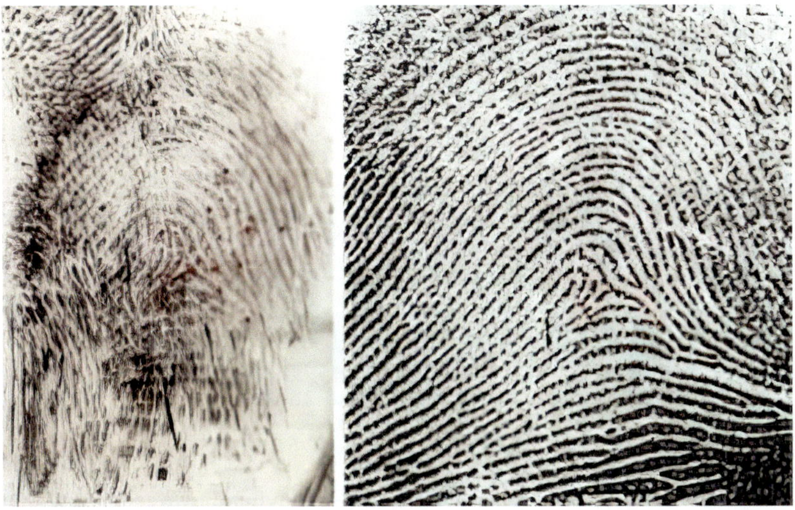

Figure 8.8 Detonator and Mayfield Prints

Source: Science Direct https://www.sciencedirect.com/science/article/pii/B978012802719600011X

partial fingerprint form the bag. The digital copy of the print was sent to the FBI, where it was compared to known prints in the AFIS database. The automated search returned 20 possible matches, including Brandon Mayfield, an attorney in Portland Oregon whose fingerprint was in the database from his eight years of service as a U.S. Army officer. An FBI fingerprint examiner compared all of the 20 prints to the print from the detonator bag and concluded that Mayfield was the source of the Madrid print. Following ACE-V procedure, a second examiner compared the two prints and also concluded that there was a match to Mayfield. The Chief of the fingerprint unit then reviewed their work and agreed that they were "100% certain" that Mayfield was the source. Based on that information, the FBI began the investigation of Mayfield (Figure 8.8).

Brandon Mayfield was a 37-year-old attorney who had grown up in Kansas and had his law degree from Washburn University in Topeka. He was married to an Egyptian woman that he had met in 1986 and converted to Islam shortly afterward. They had four children and were living in the

Figure 8.9 Brandon Mayfield

Source: Law office of Brandon Mayfield, https://mayfieldlaw.weebly.com/about.html

Portland Oregon area where he practiced law. The FBI put the family under surveillance and surreptitiously searched his office and home under the authority of a FISA warrant they had secretly obtained (Figure 8.9).

On May 4 the FBI arrested Mayfield in the family home as a "material witness" under the Patriot Act and thoroughly searched the house. He was imprisoned in the local jail and told the judge that he had never been to Spain. The FBI confirmed that he had not left the country in his name and that his passport had expired in 2003. Nevertheless the FBI claimed that he may have traveled to Madrid under a fictitious name. In court, Mayfield's attorneys asked the judge to order an independent examination of the fingerprints. The court appointed Kenneth Moses to compare the prints. Moses did so and filed an affidavit also concluding that Mayfield was a "100%" match to the print on the detonator bag.

On May 19, the same day that the Moses report was submitted, the Spanish police informed the FBI that they had positively identified the detonator fingerprint as that of a known Algerian terrorist named Ouhnane Daoud. Mayfield was released from jail, and five days later, the FBI examined Daoud's prints, and charges against Mayfield were dismissed (Figure 8.10). It turned out that back in April, the Spanish police had informed the FBI that it thought

SCIENCE OR A "LEAP OF FAITH"

Figure 8.10 Kenneth Moses

Kenneth Moses was selected as an "independent" fingerprint examiner in the case against Brandon Mayfield after three FBI examiners had stated that they were 100% certain that Mayfield was the person who had left the partial print on a detonator bag at the site of bombings in Spain that killed over 200 people. Moses examined the prints and told the Court it was a "positive match."

Source: https://www.lexvisio.com/expert-witness/kenneth-r-moses-director-forensic-id-services

Mayfield's print was not a match, but that was never disclosed to Mayfield or his attorneys (Federal Bureau of Investigation, 2004; Office of the Inspector General, 2006). Mayfield later sued the FBI and the case was settled for $2 million and an apology by the government (Lichtblau, 2006).

After Mayfield was exonerated, Moses appeared in a televised PBS Frontline episode called "The Real CSI." This is what he told PBS interviewer Lowell Bergman:

Bergman: "When you're looking at the partial print versus the known print, when do you decide it's a match? How do you decide it's a match?"

Moses: "At some point you're examining this evidence and, based upon your training and experience, *you make a leap of faith.*"

Bergman: "You make a leap of faith".
Moses: "It's a point of decision making. It's where you go from doubt to no doubt. That's a leap of faith."

Moses said that he had found 15 points of similarity between the partial and the known: "Under our past standards, I was right. But I was wrong." Frontline (2013)

8.4 WHAT DO YOU THINK?

1. Is there any connection between "faith" or "belief" and the scientific method? How would it relate to the *Daubert* criteria for reliable evidence?
2. Fingerprints and the other pattern evidence disciplines raise the important distinction between objective evidence and subjective opinion. Can you square subjective opinions based on a "leap of faith" with the need to limit admissible evidence to reliable science?

8.5 ADVANCEMENTS IN FINGERPRINT ANALYSIS

Scientists generally describe two forms of research analysis as either quantitative or qualitative. Quantitative analysis is empirical and statistical, based on verifiable data. Qualitative analysis on the other hand has an element of human opinion and subjectivity. Traditional fingerprint analysis is qualitative in the sense that it ultimately relies on the subjective conclusion of a human fingerprint examiner as to whether the questioned print and the known print came from the same person. Contrast this with the DNA analysis procedure previously described where scientists use a statistical model to estimate the likelihood that someone other than the suspect or defendant has the same DNA profile found in the crime scene evidence. Since *Daubert*, the NAS Report, research finding significant error rates, and cases like the Brandon Mayfield case, there have been efforts to move fingerprinting comparison toward a more objective and scientific quantitative basis.

While the transformation of the fingerprint identification conclusion from qualitative to quantitative is still resisted by many traditional experts, many others have proposed probabilistic frameworks. Two new models dominate those proposals. The probability of random correspondence (PRC) model is based somewhat on the AFIS (now NGI) dataset of impressions. The likelihood ratio model (LR) is also somewhat based on AFIS scores and is believed that it would allow fingerprint analysis to move closer to other evidence-based forensic disciplines. Both are based on the prevalence of the minutiae (arch, tent, whorl) within the data.

The obstacle for all of the proposals to establish a quantitative basis for fingerprint analysis is that there is not a large enough database that would provide statistical results for the various minutiae. Unlike DNA there is not yet a single database of fingerprints where the frequency of each of the smaller and more particular subsets of minutiae can be determined. Using AFIS, the frequency of tents, arches, and whorls can be roughly estimated but those broad characteristics yield an unusably large number of similar prints. Efforts are underway to develop and use a larger and more elaborate database that will someday allow analysts to make the sort of random match probabilities that are common in DNA analysis.

The development of AI may suggest a different approach altogether. It has been the fingerprinting premise, really an assumption, that human fingerprints are unique and that no two people have the same prints. Recent AI research has cast doubt on that assumption and perhaps on the way we compare prints. Using a different configuration than traditional minutiae, Columbia University researchers found that fingerprints are not necessarily unique and that, perhaps even more important, the comparison of basic minutiae like arch, tent, and whorl was not a good predictor of a common origin:

> Fingerprint biometrics are integral to digital authentication and forensic science. However, they are based on the unproven assumption that no two fingerprints, even from different fingers of the same person, are alike. This renders them useless in scenarios where the presented fingerprints are from different fingers than those on record. Contrary to this prevailing assumption, we show above 99.99% confidence that fingerprints from different fingers of the same person share very strong similarities. Using deep twin neural networks to extract fingerprint representation vectors, we find that these similarities hold across all pairs of fingers within the same person, even when controlling for spurious factors like sensor modality. We also find evidence that ridge orientation, especially near the fingerprint center, explains a substantial part of this similarity, whereas minutiae used in traditional methods are almost nonpredictive. Our experiments suggest that, in some situations, this relationship can increase forensic investigation efficiency by almost two orders of magnitude.
>
> Guo, G. et al, (2024) Unveiling intra-person fingerprint similarity via deep contrastive learning, *Science Advances*, Vol 10, Issue 2, https://doi.org/10.1126/sciadv.adi0329. DOI: 10.1126/sciadv.adi0329

If further research verifies this AI method, it could greatly enhance the predictive value of fingerprint analysis.

REFERENCES

Benedict, Nathan, *Fingerprints and the Daubert Standard for Admission of Scientific Evidence: Why Fingerprints Fail and a Proposed Remedy*, 46 Ariz. L. Rev. 519 (2004) https://www.arizonalawreview.org/pdf/46-3/46arizlrev519.pdf

Federal Bureau of Investigation, *Next Generation Identification (NGI)* (n.d.) https://le.fbi.gov/science-and-lab/biometrics-and-fingerprints/biometrics/next-generation-identification-ngi

Federal Bureau of Investigation, *Statement on Brandon Mayfield Case* (May 24, 2004) https://archives.fbi.gov/archives/news/pressrel/press-releases/statement-on-brandon-mayfield-case

Frontline, *The Real CSI*, PBS (2013) https://www.pbs.org/wgbh/frontline/documentary/real-csi/

Guo, G., et al., *Unveiling Intra-Person Fingerprint Similarity Via Deep Contrastive Learning*, 10 Sci. Adv. 2 (2024) https://www.science.org/doi/10.1126/sciadv.adi0329

Lichtblau, E., *U.S. Will Pay $2 Million to Lawyer Wrongly Jailed*, New York Times (November 30, 2006) https://www.nytimes.com/2006/11/30/us/us-will-pay-2-million-to-lawyer-wrongly-jailed.html

Mnookin, J., *The Validity of Latent Fingerprint Identification: Confessions of a Fingerprinting Moderate*, 7 Law, Prob. & Ris. 111 (2008) https://www.researchgate.net/publication/228189942_The_Validity_of_Latent_Fingerprint_Identification_Confessions_of_a_Fingerprinting_Moderate

National Research Council of the National Academies of Science, *Strengthening Forensic Science in the United States: A Path Forward* (2009) https://nap.nationalacademies.org/catalog/12589/strengthening-forensic-science-in-the-united-states-a-path-forward

Office of the Inspector General, U.S. Department of Justice, *A Review of the FBI's Handling of the Brandon Mayfield Case* (2006) https://oig.justice.gov/sites/default/files/legacy/special/s0601/exec.pdf

State v. Rose, Case No. K06-0545, Md. Balt. County, Cir. Ct. (October 19, 2007) http://www.latent-prints.com/images/State%20Of%20Maryland%20vs%20Bryan%20Rose%20K06-0545.pdf

U.S. v. Abreu, 406 F.3d 1304 (11th Cir. 2005)

U.S. v. Havvard, 260 F.3d 597 (7th Cir. 2001)

READINGS

Cole, S., *Scandal, Fraud, and the Reform of Forensic Science: The Case of Fingerprint Analysis*, 119 W. Va. L. Rev. (2016–2017) https://researchrepository.wvu.edu/wvlr/vol119/iss2/5/

Dror, E., et al., *Cognitive Issues in Fingerprint Analysis: Inter- and Intra-Expert Consistency and the Effect of a 'Target' Comparison*, 208 Forensic Sci. Int. 10 (May 20, 2011) https://doi.org/10.1016/j.forsciint.2010.10.013

Eldridge, H., *The Shifting Landscape of Latent Print Testimony: An American Perspective*, 3(2) J. Forensic Sci. Med. 72–81 (April–June 2017) https://journals.lww.com/jfsm/fulltext/2017/03020/the_shifting_landscape_of_latent_print_testimony_.6.aspx

Evarts, H., *AI Discovers That Not Every Fingerprint Is Unique*, Columbia Engineering (January 10, 2024) https://www.engineering.columbia.edu/about/news/ai-discovers-not-every-fingerprint-unique

Federal Bureau of Investigation, *Recording Legible Fingerprints*, https://le.fbi.gov/science-and-lab/biometrics-and-fingerprints/biometrics/recording-legible-fingerprints

Garrett, B., Mitchell, G. and Scurich, N., *Comparing Categorical and Probabilistic Fingerprint Evidence*, 63 J. Forensic Sci. 1712 (November 2018) https://doi.org/10.1111/1556-4029.13797

How to Compare Fingerprints, *Ray Forensics*, https://www.youtube.com/watch?v=IrpTqKkgygA

Hoy, A., *Fingerprint Source Identity Lacks Scientific Basis for Legal Certainty*, American Association for the Advancement of Science (2017) https://www.aaas.org/news/fingerprint-source-identity-lacks-scientific-basis-legal-certainty

Neumann, C. and Stern, H., *Forensic Examination of Fingerprints: Past, Present, and Future*, 29(1) Chance 9–16, Taylor & Francis (2016) https://doi.org/10.1080/09332480.2016.1156353

President's Council of Advisors on Science and Technology, *Forensic Science in Criminal Courts: Ensuring Scientific Validity of Feature Comparison Methods* (2016) https://obamawhitehouse.archives.gov/sites/default/files/microsites/ostp/PCAST/pcast_forensic_science_report_final.pdf

Stevenage, S. and Pitfield, C., *Fact or Friction: Examination of the Transparency, Reliability and Sufficiency of the ACE-V Method of Fingerprint Analysis*, 267 Forensic Sci. Int. 145 https://doi.org/10.1016/j.forsciint.2016.08.026

Ulery, B., Hicklin, R. and Buscaglia, A., *Accuracy and Reliability of Forensic Latent Fingerprint Decisions*, Proc. Nat. Acad. Sci. (2011) https://www.pnas.org/doi/10.1073/pnas.1018707108

U.S. Department of Justice, *Latent print Examination Process*, National Institute of Standards and Technology, https://ipm.nist.gov/lpe

Williams, G., McMurray, H. and Worsley, D., *Latent Fingerprint Detection Using a Scanning Kelvin Microprobe*, 46 J. Forensic Sci. 1005 (2001) https://pubmed.ncbi.nlm.nih.gov/11569547/

Worley, C., et al., *Detection of Visible and Latent Fingerprints Using Micro-X-Ray Fluorescence Elemental Imaging*, 51 J. Forensic Sci. 57 (2005) https://onlinelibrary.wiley.com/doi/abs/10.1111/j.1556-4029.2005.00006.x

9

Toolmarks and Ballistics

Toolmarks are the impressions left when a hard tool contacts a softer object. The marks may be generated during the manufacturing process, such as when the barrel of a gun is rifled by cutting tools, which leave marks on the barrel. The marks may also be generated when a manufactured item, perhaps a tool itself, is used in contact with other substances, such as when a screwdriver or crowbar is used to break into a door or window. In turn, the use of the item generates further marks on surfaces of the tool itself that were not present at the time of manufacture, such as when a gun is repeatedly fired, or a screwdriver is used over time on various other items.

Ballistics is a form of toolmark comparison, having to do with guns and ammunition. Weapons used in the commission of crimes are a prime source of evidence, as investigators seek to identify a particular gun as the source of bullets or other ammunition components. The marks made by tools in the manufacture of guns or ammunition may result in particular corresponding marks on bullets, cartridge cases, and expended shells as they process through the firing mechanism.

9.1 TOOLMARKS

A variety of tools may be used in a crime. Each tool will leave a mark on any softer surface it is used on. A harder surface may leave marks on the tool itself. Scratches, called striations, that are produced on the surface, or the tool, can then be compared to the striations produced by tests made in a laboratory by the questioned tool. The toolmark examiner will usually use a comparison microscope in the process. When a suspect tool is recovered, examiners look for distinctive features, which may be associated

DOI: 10.4324/9781041136361-11

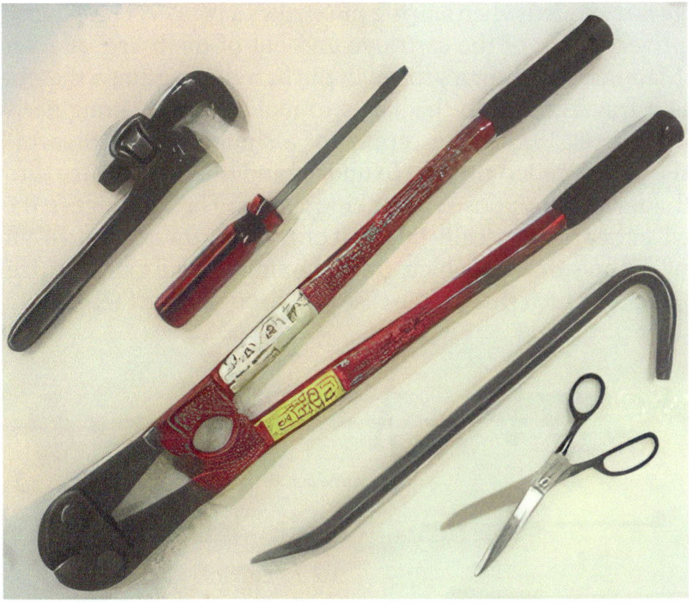

Figure 9.1 Tools.

Source: Missouri State Highway Patrol, https://apps.mshp.dps.mo.gov/MSHPWeb/PatrolDivisions/CLD/Firearms/toolmarks.html

with the individual tool. Tools like bolt cutters, screwdrivers, scissors, knives, pliers, crowbars, and saws can be examined and compared to the impressions they may have left on such things as locks, doorknobs, bolts, and many other materials (Figure 9.1).

The proffered basis for expert toolmark testimony is that each set of markings is somehow unique and such testimony has been almost always accepted. Testimony about a variety of tools has been admitted, including screwdrivers and crowbars, bolt cutters, hammers, pliers, and a punch tool. Testimony about knives has also been admitted when the knife was used as a tool.

9.2 FIREARMS

The government defines a firearm as any weapon which will expel a projectile by the action of an explosive. In all firearms, gunpowder in a cartridge is exploded when a firing pin strikes a primer. The explosion propels a projectile out of the cartridge and out of the barrel at a very high speed. Manufacturers cut a groove in the barrel of a gun so that the bullet spins as it travels through the barrel to make it travel straighter when it leaves the barrel. With the exception of a shotgun, most firearm barrels have this groove, called rifling. (To understand this concept, try throwing a football sideways as opposed to making it spin.) The cartridge in the gun is removed, either by physically taking it out of the gun or, in most automatic weapons, by an extractor which grabs the rim of the fired cartridge casing and an ejector, which throws the case out through a port (Figure 9.2).

Figure 9.2 Types of Firearms.

There are many types of firearms and the forensic examination of them and their ammunition may vary according to the type.

Source: iStock

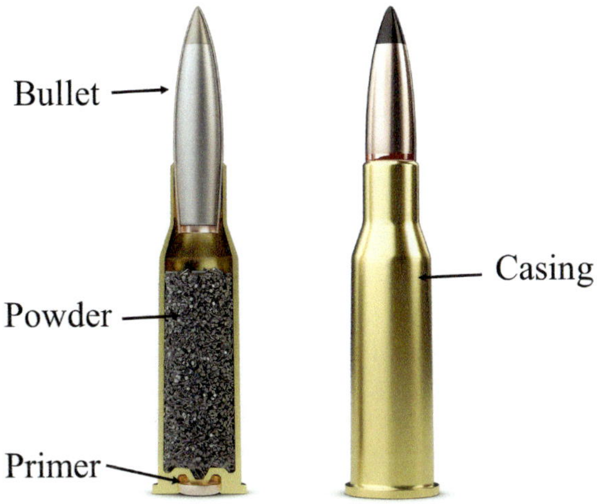

Figure 9.3 Main Components of Ammunition.

Source: iStock

The caliber of a firearm and its ammunition, other than a shotgun, refers to the diameter of the barrel and the corresponding bullet size. So, for example, the inside of the barrel of a 45 caliber pistol and its corresponding ammunition is approximately .45 inches (about 11 millimeters) in diameter. Ammunition varies according to the type of firearm, size, and type of bullet (Figure 9.3).

9.3 BALLISTICS

The ejected cartridge casings or expended bullets may be left and recovered from a crime scene. A suspect gun may later be recovered. The primary purpose of a forensic ballistics examination is to determine whether the crime scene evidence is associated with the suspect gun. There are several possible toolmarks that can be compared to make this determination.

The "rifling" that is part of the manufacturing process leaves marks and scrapes on the barrel metal. When a bullet is fired and travels through the barrel, the barrel marks are transferred to and reflected in marks, the "stria," on the fired bullet. As the gun is used repeatedly and as the barrel is cleaned, the marks in the barrel, and the resulting stria on the bullet, may develop more individual characteristics. Other individual gun characteristics can be imparted to the brass cartridge case of the bullets, as they are fired and as they are ejected from some types of guns. As the firing pin strikes the cartridge, it leaves its mark. As the cartridge case is blown back to the breech of the gun, the toolmarks in that area of the gun are impressed on the exterior of the casing. If the gun ejects the casing, the toolmarks of the extractor and ejector parts of the gun are imparted to the exterior of the casing as well.

To compare bullet striations or cartridge impressions, a recovered gun may be test fired so that the test bullet or casing can be compared to a found bullet or casing to see if they may have originated from the tested gun. As with other toolmarks, a firearms examiner makes initial visual determinations of class characteristics. The markings are then compared using a comparison microscope to see if the individual characteristics correspond (Figure 9.4).

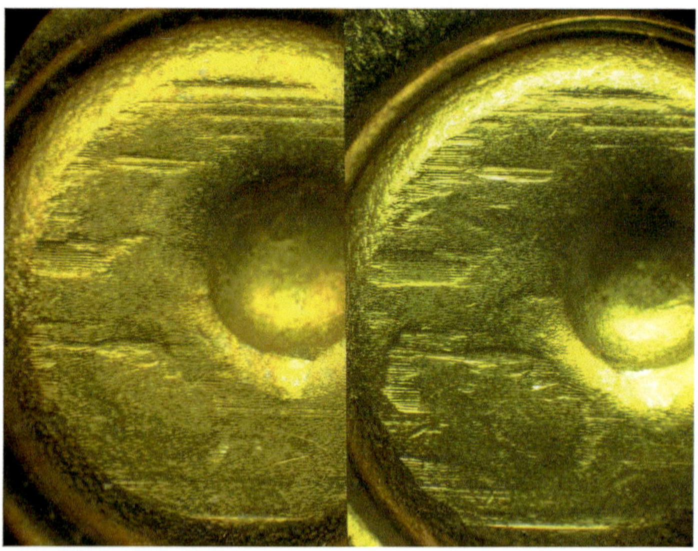

Figure 9.4 Firing Pin Mark Comparison.

NIST/Robert M. Thompson

Source: https://www.nist.gov/system/files/documents/forensics/Firearms_identity_NDAAsm.pdf

9.4 ADMISSIBILITY ISSUES

American courts have admitted firearms comparison testimony routinely for over 130 years. Any early hesitancy about its admissibility had all but disappeared by the 1930s, when the pioneer firearms scientist Calvin Goddard, perfected the comparison microscope (Goddard, 1926–1927, Figures 9.5 and 9.6).

Expert testimony that a found bullet or cartridge and a test bullet or cartridge originated from the same gun has now been admitted in every U.S. jurisdiction. However, the problems with firearms testimony are similar to the issues concerning fingerprints and other pattern identifications. They are based on questionable assumptions of uniqueness, the standards for comparison are not well established, the conclusions of the examiner are subjective and often with unsubstantiated claims of certainty (Figure 9.7).

Figure 9.5 Bullet Stria Comparison.

NIST/Robert M. Thompson

Source: **https://www.nist.gov/system/files/documents/forensics/Firearms_identity_NDAAsm.pdf**

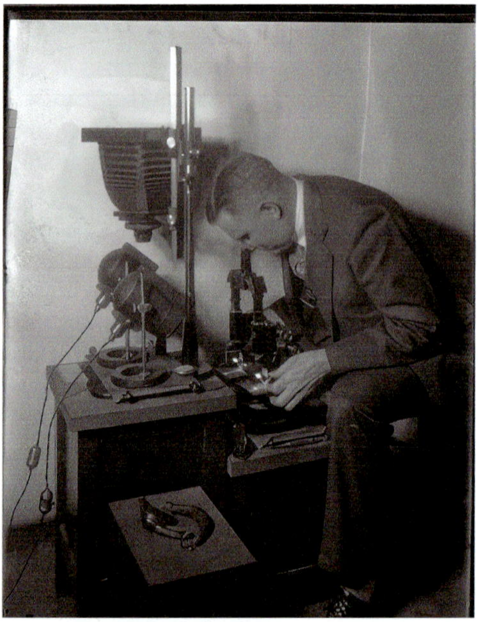

Figure 9.6 Early Comparison Microscope.

Photo by NBS/NIST; source: NARA

On the uniqueness question, an NAS 2008 Ballistics Report concluded as follows:

> The validity of the fundamental assumptions of uniqueness and reproducibility of firearms related toolmarks has not yet been fully demonstrated. . . . A significant amount of research would be needed to scientifically determine the degree to which firearms-related toolmarks are unique or even to quantitatively characterize the probability of uniqueness.
>
> National Research Council (2008) at p. 3.

The standard, or lack thereof, for determining whether the marks on two items agree is very problematic. Experts agree that there is no perfect match. The Association of Firearms and ToolMark Examiners (AFTE) states that the marks must be of "sufficient agreement" and only defines that phrase as "when it exceeds the best agreement demonstrated between toolmarks known to have been produced by different tools and is

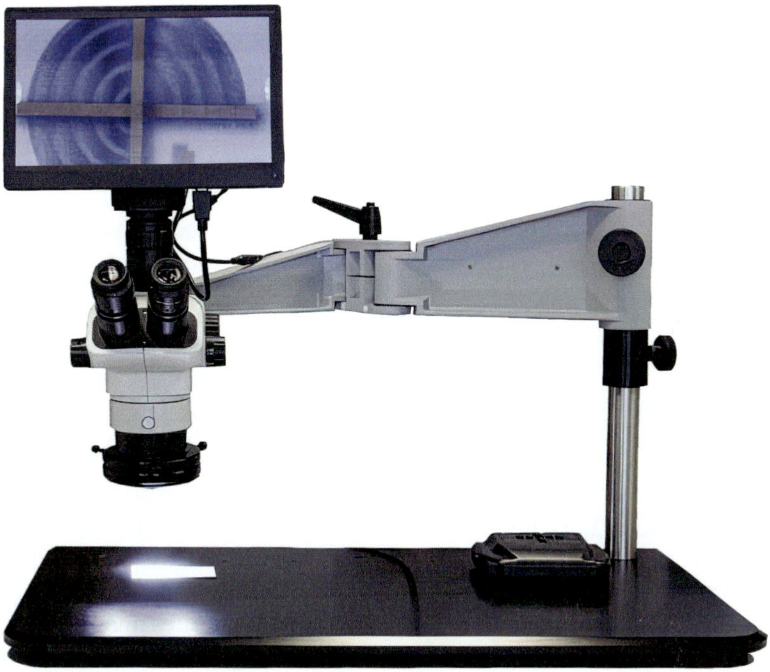

Figure 9.7 Modern Comparison Microscope.

Leeds Stereo Microscope
Source: https://www.leedsmicro.com/stereo-microscopes/

consistent with the agreement demonstrated by toolmarks known to have been produced by the same tool." (National Institute of Justice, n.d.). The circularity of this "standard," and the lack of more definite criteria, has been the subject of significant criticism (Garratt, 2023).

Like fingerprint and other impression testimony, the testimony of toolmark experts is, in the final analysis, subjective, but that alone does not render it inadmissible. The 2009 NAS Report is critical of the scientific basis for the type of toolmark and ballistics evidence that has been routinely accepted by the courts because "not enough is known about the variabilities among individual tools and guns" and because "[s]ufficient studies have not been done to understand the reliability and repeatability of the methods." National Research Council (2009) at p. 154. The Academy report found that "[a] fundamental problem with toolmark and firearms analysis is the lack of a precisely defined scientific process" and noted the "heavy reliance on the subjective findings of examiners rather than on the rigorous quantification and analysis of sources of variability." National Research Council (2009) at p. 155. However, even when confronted with the report's findings, many courts have held that ballistics testimony is admissible even without a *Daubert* hearing. Even when *Daubert* hearings or analyses are conducted, they have not resulted in many successful attacks on classic firearms expert testimony. Some recent courts have started to more critically examine ballistics testimony [Abruquah v. State, 296 A.3d 961 (Md. 2023); Balko (2025)].

9.5 ADVANCEMENTS IN FIREARMS ANALYSIS

As in other forensic science fields, the future of firearms identification expert testimony may lie in the availability of better science rather than traditional subjective judgments. In ballistics, recent advancements may lead to more scientifically based results. These advancements are primarily in the development of computerized databases of firearms and ammunition, and the development of sophisticated three-dimensional imaging processes.

The FBI developed a computerized system known as the Integrated Ballistic Identification System (IBIS) that automatically digitized and sorted bullet and shell casing characteristics:

> The ballistic comparison of crime scene bullet or cartridge casing evidence can be automatically compared with other bullet or cartridge casing images previously entered into the system. The ballistic comparison system does not positively identify (match) bullets or casings fired from the same weapon – that must be done by a firearms examiner. However, the system does produce a short list of candidates for the match. The numerical probability of a match is given for each candidate on the list eliminating the need for the examiner to visually compare unlikely candidates. By doing automated searches, the system speeds up and optimizes time spent on comparisons.
>
> U.S. Department of Justice (2011)

More recently, IBIS has been integrated into a more advanced computerized database known as the National Integrated Ballistics Information Network (NIBIN) operated by the Bureau of Alcohol, Tobacco, Firearms and Explosives (ATF). It utilizes more sophisticated algorithms and imaging and has become a system available to most law enforcement agencies. Although the ATF emphasizes that "the system does not make identifications; the firearm examiner must make the identification if two bullets or cartridge cases come from the same firearm," the automated comparison process can be a substantial step toward probabilistic based testimony rather than subjective "match" opinions (U.S. Department of Justice, 2025).

The development of new 3D imaging is paving the way for much more objectively based mathematical and statistical firearms analysis. A comparison microscope allows a flat two-dimensional view of the striations and other impressions on bullets and casings, similar to viewing a fingerprint. But the ballistics evidence we need to view is on three-dimensional objects that have depth, as well as length and width. The striations have depth. New computer systems and algorithms analyze all of the three dimensions and can convert that information into quantitative measurements that can then be statistically stated (Guarnera, 2023).

Utilizing the advantages of three-dimensional imaging, the NIST developed an algorithm known as congruent matching cells (CMCs) that compares three-dimensional scans of breech face impressions on cartridge cases. The method divides one surface into a grid of cells, then searches the other compared surface for matches. The number of matching cells produces a likelihood ratio and can make firearms comparison into a statistical for testimony that is more meaningful, and more accurate, than a subjective "match" opinion (National Institute of Standards and Technology, n.d.; Chen, 2018).

REFERENCES

Abruquah v. State, 296 A.3d 961 (Md. 2023)

Balko, R., *A Chicago Judge Just Erased Her Predecessor's Historic Ruling on Forensic Firearms Analysis*, The Watch (January 14, 2025) https://radleybalko.substack.com/p/a-chicago-judge-just-erased-her-predecessors

Chen, Z., et al., *A Normalized Congruent Matching Area Method for the Correlation of Breech Face Impression Images*, J. Res. Nat. Inst. Stand. Technol. (2018) https://tsapps.nist.gov/publication/get_pdf.cfm?pub_id=923398

Garratt, B., et al., *Judging Firearms Evidence and the Rule 702 Amendments*, 107 Judicature 2 (2023) https://judicature.duke.edu/articles/judging-firearms-evidence-and-the-rule-702-amendments/#:~:text=But%20mere%20agreement%20of%20class,at%2065

Goddard, C., *Scientific Identification of Firearms and Bullets*, 17 Am. Inst. Crim. L. Criminology 254 (1926–1927) https://scholarlycommons.law.northwestern.edu/cgi/viewcontent.cgi?article=2023&context=jclc

Guarnera, L., et al., *Assessing Forensic Ballistics Three-Dimensionally through Graphical Reconstruction and Immersive VR Observation*, 82 Multimed Tools Appl. 20655–20681 (2023) https://doi.org/10.1007/s11042-022-14037-x

National Institute of Justice, *AFTE Theory of Identification* (n.d.) https://nij.ojp.gov/nij-hosted-online-training-courses/firearms-examiner-training/module-09/afte-theory-identification

National Institute of Standards and Technology, *NIST Ballistics Toolmark Research Database*, https://tsapps.nist.gov/NRBTD/

National Research Council, *Ballistic Imaging* (2008). Washington, DC, National Acadamies Press.

National Research Council of the National Academies of Science, *Strengthening Forensic Science in the United States: A Path Forward* (2009) https://nap.nationalacademies.org/catalog/12589/strengthening-forensic-science-in-the-united-states-a-path-forward

U.S. Department of Justice, *National Integrated Ballistic Information Network (NIBIN)*, Bureau of Alcohol, Tobacco, Firearms and Explosives (ATF) (2025) https://www.atf.gov/firearms/national-integrated-ballistic-information-network-nibin

U.S. Department of Justice, *Program Profile: Integrated Ballistics Identification System (IBIS)*, National Institute of Justice (2011) https://crimesolutions.ojp.gov/ratedprograms/integrated-ballistics-identification-system-ibis#1-0

READINGS

Dorfman, A. and Valliant, R., *Inconclusives, Errors, and Error Rates in Forensic Firearms Analysis: Three Statistical Perspectives*, 8 Forensic Sci. Int. Synerg. 5 (June 2022) https://www.sciencedirect.com/science/article/pii/S2589871X22000584?via%3Dihub

Kraemer, J., *A Basic Firearm Tutorial*, American Board of Medicolegal Death Investigators (April 2009) https://abmdi.org/documents/basic_firearm_tutorial_article_april_2009_edit.pdf

LaGoo, L., *Toolmarks as Evidence*, EBSCO (2024) https://www.ebsco.com/research-starters/science/tool-marks-evidence

The Mob Museum, *The Birth of Ballistics*, https://stvalentinemassacre.org/ballistics/#full

Monson, K., Smith, E. and Bajic, S., *Planning, Design and Logistics of a Decision Analysis Study: The FBI/Ames Study Involving Forensic Firearms Examiners*, 19 Forensic Sci. Int. Synerg. 4 (February 2022) https://www.sciencedirect.com/science/article/pii/S2589871X22000067?via%3Dihub

Organization of Scientific Area Committees for Forensic Science (OSAC), *OSAC 2024-S-0002 Standard Test Method for the Examination and Comparison of Toolmarks for Source Attribution*, National Institute of Standards and Technology (NIST) (2025) https://www.nist.gov/standard/2551

Schwartz, A. (2005). *A Systemic Challenge to the Reliability and Admissibility of Firearms and Toolmark Identification*. Science and Technology Law Review, 6. https://doi.org/10.7916/stlr.v6i0.3776

Smith, A. and Wells, G., *Telling Us Less Than What They Know: Expert Inconclusive Reports Conceal Exculpatory Evidence in Forensic Cartridge-Case Comparisons*, 13 J. Appl. Res. Mem. Cogn. 147–152 (2023) https://www.researchgate.net/publication/373390356_Telling_Us_Less_Than_What_They_Know_Expert_Inconclusive_Reports_Conceal_Exculpatory_Evidence_in_Forensic_Cartridge-Case_Comparisons

U.S. Department of Justice, *Basic Toolmark Identification*, National Institute of Justice (2023) https://nij.ojp.gov/nij-hosted-online-training-courses/firearms-examiner-training/module-13/basic-toolmark-identification#:~:text=Striated%20toolmarks%20(also%20called%20striae,the%20discharge%20of%20a%20firearm

U.S. Department of Justice, *A Century of Ballistics Comparison Giving Way to Virtual 3D Methods*, National Institute of Justice (2022) https://nij.ojp.gov/topics/articles/century-ballistics-comparison-giving-way-virtual-3d-methods

Warlow, T., *Firearms, the Law, and Forensic Ballistics* (2d ed., 2004). CRC Press. https://doi.org/10.1201/9780203568224

Zhu, J., et al., *The Reliability of Forensic Evidence: The Case of Curtis Flowers*, Cornell Univ. Law School, https://courses2.cit.cornell.edu/sociallaw/FlowersCase/forensicevidence.html

10

Handwriting

Questioned Document Examination

10.1 HANDWRITING ANALYSIS

Handwriting analysis involves the comparison of a questioned handwritten item with an item of known origin. Certain requirements must be met before a handwriting comparison can be made. The writing must be of the same type (e.g., handwritten or hand printed) and the text must be of a comparable sort (e.g., similar letter and word combinations). Special situations involve forgery, which is an attempt to imitate another's writing, and disguise, which is an attempt to change writing style to prevent identification.

The bases for comparison are the features or attributes that are common to both samples. Similar to other pattern identifications, the characteristics of the writings are identified as class characteristics (the style that the writer was taught), individual characteristics (the writer's personal style), and other gross or subtle characteristics. The attributes used for comparison of handwriting are 21 so-called discriminating elements.

Handwriting comparison is based on the principle that, although individuals have variations within their own writing, no two persons write the same way. The analysis compares variability among writers and variability within a single person's writing, as shown in the samples. Determining that two samples were written by the same person means that the handwriting examiner has subjectively concluded that the degree of variability is more consistent with individual writing variations than with variations

DOI: 10.4324/9781041136361-12

between two different persons. Professor D. Michael Risinger summed up the contentions of the handwriting analysts:

> Handwriting identification experts believe they can examine a specimen of adult handwriting and determine whether the author of that specimen is the same person as or a different person than the author of any other example of handwriting, as long as both specimens are of sufficient quality and not separated by years or the intervention of degenerative disease. They further believe that they can accomplish this result with great accuracy, and that they can do it much better than an average literate person attempting the same task. They believe they can obtain these accurate findings as the result of applying an analytical methodology to the examination of handwriting, according to certain principles which are reflected in the questioned documents literature. They believe that this literature explains how to examine handwriting for identifying characteristics, and that by applying the lessons taught by this literature in connection with their experiences in various training exercises and in real world problems, they learn to identify handwriting dependably.
>
> Risinger (2013) at pp. 590–591

10.2 ADMISSIBILITY ISSUES

Although early American courts rejected the idea of handwriting comparison as admissible forensic science evidence, the tide turned in State v. Hauptmann, 115 N.J.L. 412, 180 A. 809 (N.J. Ct. Err. & App. 1935), the very famous Lindbergh kidnapping case. Albert Osborne was the primary proponent of handwriting comparison and was the chief prosecution witness in the trial of the alleged kidnapper (Sellers, 1947–1948). In the next 50 years, American courts have almost universally accepted and admitted handwriting comparison testimony in evidence.

Following *Daubert* and *Kumho*, and later the NAS Report, courts began to reevaluate the admissibility of handwriting comparison testimony. In 1995, prior to *Kumho*, the judge in U.S. v. Starzecpyzel, 880 F. Supp. 1027, 42 Fed. R. Evid. Serv. 247 (S.D. N.Y. 1995) found that handwriting comparison testimony was not a reliable science under *Daubert* standards but then said *Daubert* did not apply because handwriting was not a "science." The subsequent *Kumho* case obviously changed that distinction. Other judges then began to doubt, and exclude or limit handwriting comparison testimony [U.S. v. Fujii, 152 F. Supp.2d 939 (N.D. Ill. 2000); U.S. v. Saelee, 162 F. Supp.2d 1097 (D. Alaska 2001); Risinger (2007–2008)]. Nevertheless, many courts continue to routinely admit handwriting comparison testimony, exemplified by the approach in U.S. v. Crisp, 324 F.3d 261 (4th Cir. 2003), which treated a challenge to handwriting similar to a challenge to fingerprint comparison testimony (See the discussion of the *Crisp* reliance on precedent in Chapter 4).

The NAS Report found value in handwriting comparison testimony but recommended further scientific study:

> The scientific basis for handwriting comparisons needs to be strengthened. Recent studies have increased our understanding of the individuality and consistency of handwriting and computer studies and suggest that there may be a scientific basis for handwriting comparison, at least in the absence of intentional obfuscation or forgery. Although there has been only limited research to quantify the reliability and replicability of the practices used by trained document examiners, the committee agrees that there may be some value in handwriting analysis.
>
> National Research Council (2009) at pp. 166–167

The basic principles of handwriting analysis are generally accepted as plausible scientific hypotheses. However, scientists point out that this plausibility is based on intuition rather than scientifically established evidence. Determining whether each person's handwriting is truly unique would necessitate a study of a large number of randomly chosen persons and the categorization and measurement of the multitude of possible variations.

In 2022, the American Academy of Forensic Sciences Standards Board adopted what is called "Standard for Examination of Handwritten Items." The document does set forth procedures handwriting examiners should follow, but each of the procedures relies entirely on the subjective opinion of the examiner. It concludes that the "examiner shall form a conclusion for each set of comparisons with respect to the results of the above procedures and report accordingly." American Academy of Forensic Sciences (2022) at p. 13. The lack of quantifiable data about handwriting means that any conclusion of a handwriting examiner is "qualitative," a euphemism for subjective.

> A handwriting examination involves human perceptions and interpretation of the similarities and differences among the questioned writing and "standards" or "exemplars" from known individuals.
>
> National Institute of Standards and Technology (2021) at p. 33

As with most other pattern identification, handwriting examiner testimony is subjective and therefore depends on the proficiency of the particular examiner. The error rate is an important element of a *Daubert* analysis of the reliability of handwriting comparison evidence. The FBI undertook a five-year study to assess the accuracy and reliability of forensic handwriting comparisons, using 86 examiners and hundreds of comparisons. The error rate for "false positives," erroneous conclusions that the document was written by the suspect, was 3.1%. The error rate for "false negatives," wrongfully concluding that the document was not written by the suspect, was 1.1% (Hicklin, 2022). There are obvious limitations to the study, including the small number of participants and the participant selection process, but at least as far as the study goes, the error rate appears to be relatively small. Other studies have cast doubt on these rates based on potential cognitive bias by handwriting examiners (Dror, 2021).

10.3 ADVANCEMENTS IN HANDWRITING COMPARISON

Some significant advancements have been made in the effort to establish a more scientific basis for testimony about questioned documents. The principal prospect for such evidence may lie in recent efforts to use computer analysis to compile quantifiable features and characteristics and to compile a database for statistical comparison.

New software programs assist in the computerized comparison of handwriting. "Flash ID" was developed by the Sciometrics company and is used by the FBI (Sciometrics, n.d.). Flash ID is a scanned image-based program that segments the writing into "graphemes" of shape and class characteristics. The program algorithms compare the graphemes rhemes of the questioned and known writings and can express them in terms of statistical likelihood. It is a totally automated process that extracts graphical data and then analyzes it with statistical methods and then matches documents based on their similarity. It is a significant step forward. Other related programs have also been developed (Srihari, 2013).

CASE STUDY The Lindbergh Kidnapping

Following his historic nonstop flight from New York to Paris in 1927, Charles Lindbergh became of the most famous persons in the world. His marriage two years later and the birth of their first son, Charles, were big news. However, in 1932, the 20-month-old Charles was kidnapped from the Lindbergh home and the case was quickly dubbed the "Crime of the Century." Over two years later, a German immigrant, Bruno Richard Hauptmann, was arrested. At his trial much of the prosecution case hinged on the testimony of experts in the fledgling forensic science field of handwriting comparison (Figure 10.1).

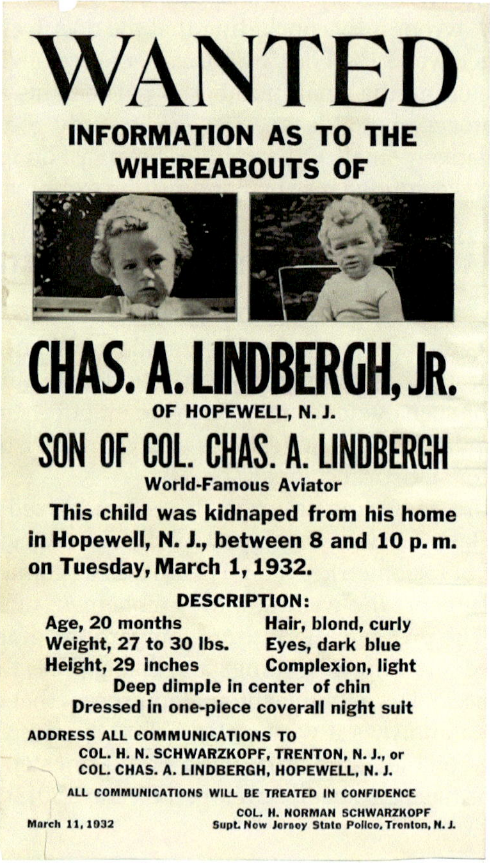

Figure 10.1 Kidnapping Poster.

Source: Minnesota Historical Society https://www.mnhs.org/lindbergh/learn/kidnapping

On March 1, 1932, using a homemade ladder, someone climbed into the second-story nursery of the Lindbergh home in New Jersey and abducted the infant. A three-piece wooden ladder, a chisel, and a handwritten ransom note demanding $50,000 were left at the scene. Five days later, a second ransom note was received, increasing the ransom demand to $70,000. A third ransom note was received by the Lindbergh's attorney, and a fourth ransom note was received by a person who had publicly offered to act as an intermediary, Dr. Condon. A fifth ransom note was delivered to him by a taxicab driver, who received it from an unidentified stranger. A sixth note led the intermediary to meet an unidentified man at a New York City cemetery. The stranger eventually gave him a baby's sleeping suit, which was identified by the Lindberghs. Negotiations continued, and a total of 13 ransom notes were delivered. Finally, the intermediary met an unidentified man and gave him $50,000 in exchange for the 13th note, which contained instructions on where to find the child. Most of the money was paid in "gold certificates," a form of U.S. currency still used at the time, and the numbers on the certificates had been recorded. The Lindbergh baby was not where the kidnapper had indicated. On May 12, 1932, the child's partially decomposed remains were found in a shallow grave just two miles from the Lindbergh home.

Over two years later, one of the $10 gold certificates from the ransom money was used at a gas station in New York and the attendant noted the license plate number. The car was traced to Bruno Hauptmann, who also had another bill of the ransom money in his possession when he was arrested. In a subsequent search of Hauptmann's garage, police found $14,000 more of the ransom money.

The 1935 sensational trial took place in a New Jersey state court and lasted six weeks. Eight government handwriting experts testified, including Albert Osborn, the man who had championed handwriting analysis as a forensic science. They testified that Hauptmann had written the ransom notes, although they did not identify him as the writer of the original note left at the scene. They claimed that Hauptmann's handwriting had many points of similarity with the ransom notes. For example, both Hauptmann's handwriting and that found on the ransom notes had backward "N"s, unclosed "o"s, the same shaped "t"s, and the same curls to the "y"s. They also testified that Hauptmann misspelled many of the same words that were misspelled in the ransom notes (Figure 10.2). For example, Hauptmann and the author of

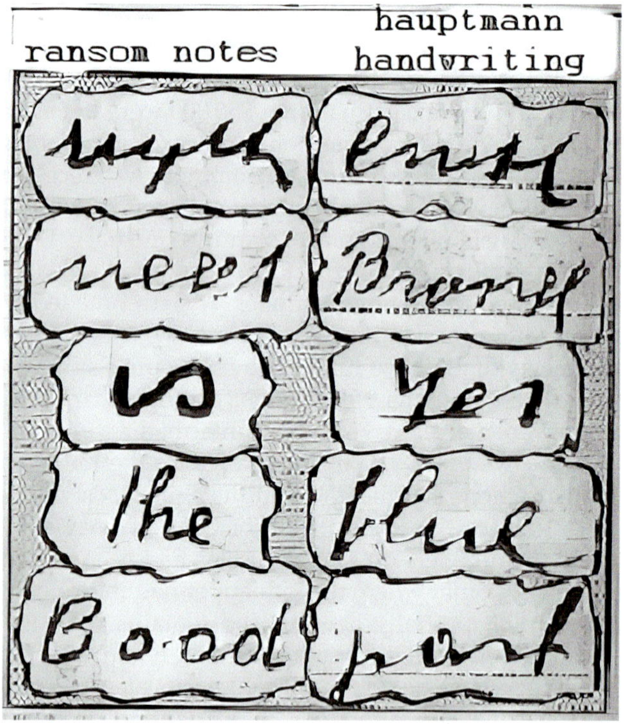

Figure 10.2 Hauptman Handwriting Evidence.

Source: UMKC School of Law, https://www.famous-trials.com/hauptmann/1396-images

the ransom notes both misspelled "where" as "were," "our" as "ouer," "later" as "latter," and "boat" as "boad."

The judge allowed all of the handwriting witnesses to testify and later instructed the jury:

> A very important question in the case is, did the defendant, Hauptmann, write the original ransom note found on the window sill, and the other ransom notes which followed? Numerous experts in handwriting have testified, after exhaustive examination of the ransom letters, and comparison with genuine writings of the defendant, that the defendant, Hauptmann, wrote every one of the ransom notes, and Mr. Osborne, Senior, said that that conclusion was irresistible, unanswerable and

overwhelming. On the other hand, the defendant denies that he wrote them, and a handwriting expert, called by him, so testified. And so the fact becomes one for your determination. The weight of the evidence to prove the genuineness of handwriting is wholly for the jury.

The jury found Bruno Richard Hauptmann guilty of first-degree murder and sentenced him to death. The conviction was upheld on appeal and Hauptmann was executed on April 3, 1936, still proclaiming his innocence.

REFERENCES

American Academy of Forensic Sciences (AAFS), *Standard for Examination of Handwritten Items*, Academy Standards Board (2022) https://www.aafs.org/sites/default/files/media/documents/070_Std_e1.pdf

Dror, I., et al., *Biasability and Reliability of Expert Forensic Document Examiners*, 318 Forensic Sci. Int. (2021) https://www.sciencedirect.com/science/article/pii/S0379073820304722

Hicklin, R., et al., *Accuracy and Reliability of Forensic Handwriting Comparisons*, Proceedings of the National Academy of Sciences (PNAS) (2022) https://www.pnas.org/doi/10.1073/pnas.2119944119

National Institute of Standards and Technology, *Forensic Handwriting Examination and Human Factors: Improving the Practice Through a Systems Approach* (2021) https://nvlpubs.nist.gov/nistpubs/ir/2021/NIST.IR.8282r1.pdf

National Research Council of the National Academies of Science, *Strengthening Forensic Science in the United States: A Path Forward* (2009), p. 185. https://nap.nationalacademies.org/catalog/12589/strengthening-forensic-science-in-the-united-states-a-path-forward

Risinger, D. M., *Cases Involving the Reliability of Handwriting Identification Expertise Since the Decision, in Daubert Symposium: Daubert, Innocence, and the Future of Forensic Science*, 43 Tulsa L. Rev. (2007–2008)

Risinger, D. M., *Handwriting Identification*, chapter 34 in *Modern Scientific Evidence, 2013–2014*, Faigman, D., Kaye, D., Saks, M., and Sanders, J. (Eds.) (2023). Thomson Reuters.

Sciometrics, *FlashID - Advanced Handwriting Identification Tool* (n.d.) https://www.sciometrics.com/product-flashid.html

Sellers, C., *Albert S. Osborn*, 38 J. Crim. L. Criminology 75 (1947–1948) https://scholarlycommons.law.northwestern.edu/cgi/viewcontent.cgi?article=3457&context=jclc

Srihari, S., *Statistical Examination of Handwriting Characteristics using Automated Tools*, U.S. Department of Justice (2013) https://www.ojp.gov/library/publications/statistical-examination-handwriting-characteristics-using-automated-tools

State v. Hauptmann, 115 N.J.L. 412, 180 A. 809 (N.J. Ct. Err. & App. 1935)
U.S. v. Crisp, 324 F.3d 261 (4th Cir. 2003)
U.S. v. Fujii, 152 F. Supp.2d 939 (N.D. Ill. 2000)
U.S. v. Saelee, 162 F. Supp.2d 1097 (D. Alaska 2001)
U.S. v. Starzecpyzel, 880 F. Supp. 1027, 42 Fed. R. Evid. Serv. 247 (S.D. N.Y. 1995)

READINGS

Crot, S. and Marquis, R., *A Comparative Review of Error Rates in Forensic Handwriting Examination*, 69 J. Forensic Sci. 6 (2024) https://onlinelibrary.wiley.com/doi/10.1111/1556-4029.15589

Kam, M., Wetstein, J. and Conn, R., *Proficiency of Professional Document Examiners in Writer Identification*, 39 J. Forensic Sci. 1 (1994) https://dl.astm.org/jofs/article-abstract/39/1/5/25414/Proficiency-of-Professional-Document-Examiners-in?redirectedFrom=fulltext

Kam, M., et al., *Signature Authentication by Forensic Document Examiners*, 46 J. Forensic Sci. 4 (2001) https://pubmed.ncbi.nlm.nih.gov/11451071/

Layton, J., *How Handwriting Analysis Works*, HowStuffWorks (2023) https://science.howstuffworks.com/handwriting-analysis.htm

Linder, D., *Hauptmann (Lindbergh) Trial*, University of Missouri Kansas City Law School (1935) https://www.famous-trials.com/hauptmann

Martire, K. A., Growns, B. and Navarro, D. J., *What Do the Experts Know? Calibration, Precision, and the Wisdom of Crowds among Forensic Handwriting Experts*, 25 Psychon. Bull. Rev. 2346–2355 (2018) https://doi.org/10.3758/s13423-018-1448-3

Risinger, D. M., *Handwriting Identification, in Modern Scientific Evidence: The Law and Science of Expert Testimony* , Slobogin., C., Faigman, D., Cheng, E., Murphy, E., Mnookin, J., and Sanders, J. (Eds.). Thomson Reuters. (1989).

Risinger, D. M., Denbeaux, M. and Saks, M., *Exorcism of Ignorance as a Proxy for Rational Knowledge: The Lessons of Handwriting Identification "Expertise"*, 137 U. Pa. L. Rev. 731 (1989) https://scholarship.law.upenn.edu/cgi/viewcontent.cgi?article=3835&context=penn_law_review

Srihari, S., et al., *Individuality of Handwriting*, 47 J. Forensic Sci. 4 (2002) https://pubmed.ncbi.nlm.nih.gov/12136998/

11

Digital Forensics

11.1 DIGITAL EVIDENCE

Digital forensics is the analysis of electronic information that is stored or transmitted in binary form, including such places as a computer hard drive, a mobile phone, a flash drive, and many other devices. In the criminal justice context, it may be evidence of a crime that was committed electronically, such as credit card or other fraud, but more often, it is substantive evidence that is relevant to other crimes, such as the suspect's location, communications, or image or audio recordings. The data from electronic devices is often recoverable because the data leaves digital traces, or footprints, on the device or on the Internet. Social media posts often contain user and location data that may be relevant evidence. Mobile devices are a widely used source for digital evidence because they store information about locations and times, especially when used in connection with information on satellite navigation systems. As we rely more on computer systems and the Internet, we conduct much of our lives online through an increasing number and types of digital devices. Every connected electronic device generates data. In addition to personal devices like mobile phones and computers, data may come from public devices like traffic lights or closed-circuit video cameras. The result is more data everywhere, and the police want to use that digital evidence to investigate and document criminal activity. They can use a wide range of digital forensics tools, including hardware and software that can analyze data without modifying it (Figure 11.1).

DOI: 10.4324/9781041136361-13

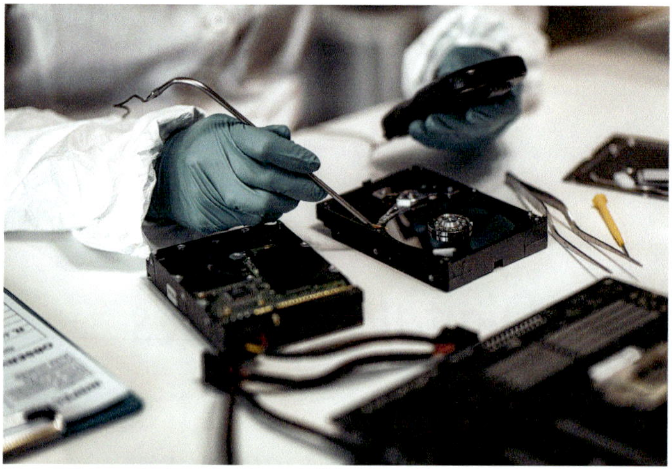

Figure 11.1 Digital Evidence Examination.

Source: iStock

11.2 SEIZURE OF DIGITAL EVIDENCE

Electronic devices have become ubiquitous to the point where at least 95% of American households have at least one computer and 98% of Americans have and use a mobile phone. These devices contain so much personal information that police acquisition of that information can raise significant privacy issues. Law enforcement may clearly search such devices if they get a search warrant based on probable cause that a crime has been committed. But searching an electronic device without a warrant, such as incident to an arrest, is prohibited by the Fourth Amendment protection against unreasonable search and seizure. In Riley v. California, 573 U.S. 373 (2014), the Supreme Court held that police may not, without a warrant, search digital information on a cell phone seized from an individual who has been arrested.

> Modern cell phones are not just another technological convenience. With all they contain and all they may reveal, they hold for many Americans "the privacies of life". The fact that technology now allows an individual to carry such information in his hand

> does not make the information any less worthy of the protection for which the Founders fought. Our answer to the question of what police must do before searching a cell phone seized incident to an arrest is accordingly simple – get a warrant.
>
> U.S. Supreme Court, Riley v. California (2014)

Based on similar privacy concerns, the Supreme Court also held in United States v. Jones, 565 U.S. 400 (2012), that the police, even with a search warrant, may not attach a digital tracking device to a suspect's vehicle. As to computers, a warrant allowing seizure of the computer does not necessarily allow a search of the information on the device without particular authorization in the warrant. There are also significant concerns when the government conducts an online search, which is a means of investigation that allows the remote access to a digital device by creating a link that can monitor all the user's activities. And the Supreme Court held in Carpenter v. United States, 585 U.S. 296 (2018), that individuals can keep a right to private cell phone data even though that same information was already disclosed to their cell phone companies. *Carpenter* may mean that some sensitive digital information, even if it is already in the possession of a third party, will require a search warrant from a judge (Figure 11.2).

11.3 ADMISSIBILITY ISSUES

Beyond search questions, there are basic general evidence requirements that are specific to digital evidence. First, digital evidence is highly volatile and fragile. The storage media and its intangible nature may make it susceptible to accidental alteration or manipulation that can affect authenticity. The chain of custody of the data, and not just the device, is essential to its admissibility.

The application of the *Daubert* criteria to digital evidence may present some reliability issues. When the software used to analyze digital evidence is commercially produced, its owners may resist efforts to allow disclosure of its source codes that would allow a court to determine what standards, if any, were used in the analysis. For open-source software that is publicly available, it can make the *Daubert* standards and testing criteria more available.

Figure 11.2 Searching the Contents of a Computer.

Source: Freepik

A great deal of digital forensics analysis has now been standardized. The International Organization for Standardization has published guidelines for acquisition, preservation, and analysis of digital evidence in a variety of situations (International Organization for Standardization, 2012). Extracting digital evidence from a mobile device is different than a computer hard drive, and specific procedures are required.

Similarly, the testing and error rate criteria of *Daubert* have been addressed for particular analysis tools. In the United States, the NIST tests many products and provides the basis for asserting that the data gathered and analyzed by new tools is scientifically valid. The NIST Computer Forensic Tool Testing project has established a methodology for testing computer forensic software tools to ensure that they consistently produce accurate and objective test results (National Institute of Standards and Technology, 2025). NIST operates the National Software Reference Library, which collects software that has been tested and can be used by law enforcement (National Institute of Standards and Technology, 2022). The NIST test results are publicly available.

Figure 11.3 Training Forensic Science Analysts.

Source: iStock

Whether the digital analysis has been correctly applied to a particular case involves examination of the analyst's expertise. Commercial forensic analysis software vendors have made significant improvements in their methodologies so that they can now be used by persons without many years of experience or training. While that is useful for police agencies, it may pose testimonial issues when those less trained analysts appear in court (Figure 11.3).

REFERENCES

Carpenter v. United States, 585 U.S. 296 (2018)

International Organization for Standardization, *Information Technology — Security Techniques — Guidelines for Identification, Collection, Acquisition and Preservation of Digital Evidence* (2012) https://amnafzar.net/files/1/ISO%2027000/ISO%20 IEC%2027037-2012.pdf

National Institute of Standards and Technology, *National Software Reference Library (NSRL)* (2022) https://www.nist.gov/itl/ssd/software-quality-group/national-software-reference-library-nsrl
National Institute of Standards and Technology, *Computer Forensics Tool Testing Program (CFTT)* (2025) https://www.nist.gov/itl/ssd/software-quality-group/computer-forensics-tool-testing-program-cftt
Riley v. California, 573 U.S. 373 (2014)
U.S. v. Jones, 565 U.S. 400 (2012)

READINGS

Authentication of Digital Evidence, Institute of Forensic Auditors, https://ifaglobal.institute/blog/authentication-of-digital-evidence
Berman, E., *Digital Searches, the Fourth Amendment, and the Magistrates' Revolt*, 68 Emory L. J. 49 (2018) https://scholarlycommons.law.emory.edu/elj/vol68/iss1/2
Carranza, A. and DeCusatis, C., *Software Validation and Daubert Standard Compliance of an Open Digital Forensics Model*, 2 Journal of Machine Intelligence and Data Science (JMIDS) 33 (2021) https://jmids.avestia.com/2021/005.html
Garrie, D. and Morrissy, J., *Digital Forensic Evidence in the Courtroom: Understanding Content and Quality*, 12 Nw. J. Tech. Intell. Prop. 121 (2014) https://scholarlycommons.law.northwestern.edu/njtip/vol12/iss2/5/
Kessler, G. C. and Carlton, G. H., *Exploring Myths in Digital Forensics: Separating Science from Ritual*, 9(4) Int. J. Interdiscip. Telecommun. Netw. (2017) https://doi.org/10.4018/IJITN.2017100101
Meyers, M. and Rogers, M., *Digital Forensics: Meeting the Challenges of Scientific Evidence*, chapter in *Advances in Digital Forensics. Vol 194: IFIP – the International Federation for Information Processing*, Pollitt, M. and Shenoi, S. (Eds.), Boston, MA, Springer (2006) https://doi.org/10.1007/0-387-31163-7_4
Murphy, M., *Digital Forensic Evidence*, Coastal Carolina University, https://ww2.coastal.edu/mmurphy2/oer/forensics/law/evidence/
Robinton, L., *Courting Chaos: Conflicting Guidance from Courts Highlights the Need for Clearer Rules to Govern the Search and Seizure of Digital Evidence*, 12 Yale J. L. Tech. 311 (2010) https://yjolt.org/courting-chaos-conflicting-guidance-courts-highlights-need-clearer-rules-govern-search-and-seizure
Singh, G., *The Five Rules of Digital Forensic Evidence*, YouTube, https://youtu.be/Uo7wu4lBJRE?si=fBk3RxiFOLZmOQjh
Software Quality Group, *National Software Reference Library (NSRL)*, National Institute of Standards and Technology (2022) https://www.nist.gov/itl/ssd/software-quality-group/national-software-reference-library-nsrl

Software Quality Group, *Computer Forensics Tool Testing Program (CFTT)*, National Institute of Standards and Technology (2025) https://www.nist.gov/itl/ssd/software-quality-group/computer-forensics-tool-testing-program-cftt

Tokson, M., *The Impact of Carpenter v. United States in the Lower Courts and the Emerging Carpenter Test*, Lawfare Institute (2021) https://www.lawfaremedia.org/article/impact-carpenter-v-united-states-lower-courts-and-emerging-carpenter-test#:~:text=The%20Supreme%20Court's%202018%20decision,to%20their%20cell%20phone%20companies

12

Footwear Comparison

12.1 FOOTWEAR IMPRESSIONS

Crime scene investigators need to be very careful not to disturb any footwear impressions that may be at or near the scene. While some footprints may be visible because they are left in dirt, mud, blood, or some other material, many may be latent and need some artificial means to be observed. Special light sources can reveal patent or latent footprints. Electrostatic lifting devices use static electricity to lift a latent impression to a black film. Dusting a footprint using material similar to fingerprint dusting can also reveal a latent footprint that can be lifted and preserved. Bloody latent footprints can be made visible by the use of chemical agents like luminol or a protein called Amino Black. If the impression is three dimensional, such as a footprint in mud, a cast can be made with plaster or dental stone. Footprints in snow pose significant issues since casting and other physical or chemical techniques may destroy the impression. Recent developments in three-dimensional image scanning and development of a three-dimensional model have been effectively used to preserve impressions in snow or sand.

12.2 FOOTWEAR IDENTIFICATION AND COMPARISON

Initial identification of the model of the shoe or other footwear that left an impression at a crime scene is made with the use of large commercially available databases. These databases contain extensive information about various types of footwear. Comparison of a shoe print with the data in the database can make an identification of the make and model of the

DOI: 10.4324/9781041136361-14

shoe. The NIST maintains a Footwear Impression Comparison System (National Institute of Standards and Technology, 2020). Many agencies use "Solemate FPX," which is a searchable database with over 42,000 footwear items (Foster + Freeman, n.d.).

Comparison of the impression with a collected shoe of a suspect is the crucial part of the footwear examination. Simple observations and measurements can determine if the model and size are the same. Beyond that, the validity of a comparison will depend in large part on the wear characteristics of the footwear. Footwear gradually acquires wear and tear on the sole, and these acquired characteristics may provide a link between the impression and the suspect footwear. These characteristics may be cuts, scratches, gouges, holes, or substances like chewing gum (Figure 12.1),

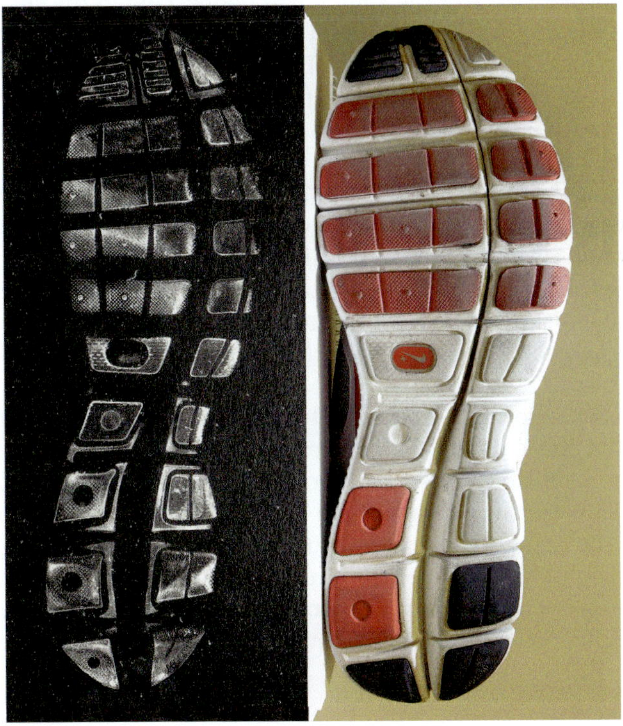

Figure 12.1 Shoeprint Comparison.

Source: Wikimedia Commons https://commons.wikimedia.org/wiki/File:Shoeprint_comparison.jpg

12.3 ADMISSIBILITY ISSUES

While footwear comparison may provide good investigational information, especially in the exclusion of certain footwear, its admissibility in court as evidence of identification may be problematic. Like many forms of pattern identification evidence, courts traditionally have allowed footwear examiners to give their subjective opinions about whether footwear from the defendant left the impression at the crime scene. U.S. v. Mason, 662 F. Supp. 3d 548 (D. Maryland 2023)

Footwear examiners have variously described their conclusions as a "match" or "consistent with." However, analysis using the *Daubert* criteria has cast doubt on such testimony.

As for error rates, a 2022 Interpol study found that footprint examiners were correct 94.5% of the time when they excluded the suspect shoe, but only 85% were correct when they identified the suspect shoe as creating the impression (Charron, 2023). The biggest issue with footwear comparison, as with other pattern identifications, is the lack of standards and the subjectivity of the analysis. The 2009 NAS Report found that "there is no defined threshold that must be surpassed, nor are there any studies that associate the number of matching characteristics with the probability that the impressions were made by a common source." The subjectivity of the opinions is related to the training and proficiency of the individual examiner. The NAS Report stated that the "educational background of forensic scientists who examine shoeprints . . . runs the gamut from a high school diploma to scientists with Ph.D.s." National Research Council (2009) at p. 146.

Significant efforts have been made to move away from this total subjectivity and to create databases and programs that will provide a statistical basis for probabilistic testimony if footwear comparison analysis. First, the advancements in three-dimensional imaging have greatly enhanced the quality of the crime scene footwear impressions. Equally important, databases and computerized algorithms have been developed that can compare the incidence of characteristics, especially of the wear and tear marks, to a general population of shoeprints acquired for a variety of sources.

REFERENCES

Charron, J., et al., *Interpol Review Paper of Marks and Impression Evidence 2019–2022*, Forensic Sci. Int. Synerg. Vol. 6 (2023) https://doi.org/10.1016/j.fsisyn.2022.100308

Foster + Freeman, *Solemate FPX Footwear Print Identification System* (n.d.) https://photonlines-forensic.fr/wp-content/uploads/2016/06/SoleMate_FPX_brochure.pdf

National Institute of Standards and Technology, *NIST Footwear Impression Comparison System* (2020) https://www.nist.gov/system/files/documents/2020/12/08/Forensics%40NIST2020-Slides-Statistics%20%281%29.pdf

National Research Council of the National Academies of Science, *Analysis of Hair Evidence, Strengthening Forensic Science in the United States: A Path Forward* (2009) https://nap.nationalacademies.org/catalog/12589/strengthening-forensic-science-in-the-united-states-a-path-forward

U.S. v. Mason, 662 F. Supp.3d 548 (D. Maryland 2023)

READINGS

Bodziak, W., *Footwear Impression Evidence Detection, Recovery and Examination,* 2d ed., Boca Raton, FL, CRC Press (2000).

Chapman, R., et al., *Novices Cannot Fill the Examiners' Shoes: Evidence of Footwear Examiners' Expertise in Shoe Comparisons,* 63 Science & Justice 5 (2023) https://www.sciencedirect.com/science/article/pii/S1355030623000825

Gross, S., *Footwear Impression Evidence.* Florida International University, https://archive.gfjc.fiu.edu/ipes/presentations/Gross_shoeprint-daubert.pdf

Hicklin, R., et al., *Accuracy, Reproducibility, and Repeatability of Forensic Footwear Examiner Decisions,* 339 Forensic Sci. Int. (2022) https://www.sciencedirect.com/science/article/pii/S0379073822002481

McMillion, M., *3D Documentation of Footwear Impressions at Crime Scenes in Minutes, No Contact Needed,* Artec 3D, https://www.artec3d.com/cases/3d-scanning-footwear-impressions-for-forensics

Sauerwein, K., *Summary of Published Criticisms of Footwear and Tire Impression Examination and Responses,* National Institute of Standards and Technology (2024) https://nvlpubs.nist.gov/nistpubs/ir/2024/NIST.IR.8509sup2.pdf

A Simplified Guide To Footwear & Tire Track Examination, *Forensic Science Simplified,* https://www.forensicsciencesimplified.org/fwtt/FootwearTireTracks.pdf

Venkatasubramanian G, et al., *Comparing Footwear Impressions That Are Close Non-Matches using Correlation-Based Approaches,* 66 J. Forensic Sci. 3 (2021) https://pubmed.ncbi.nlm.nih.gov/33682930/

Part III

The Admissibility of "How" Testimony

13

Fire and Explosions

The primary use of forensic science evidence relating to fires is to attempt to identify the source of the fire and to determine whether and what type of an accelerant was used to start or spread a fire. Arson investigations focus on the cause of a fire, often looking for the presence of an accelerant. The presence of an accelerant is most often detected by its odor, and investigators use dogs or commercial electronic sniffers to detect the areas for possible investigation. Gasoline or other petroleum-based products are the dominant form of accelerants used in intentionally set fires. Once an accelerant is detected, fire debris is examined in the laboratory to identify common petroleum-based products using gas chromatography

Forensic investigation of explosions and explosive devices focuses on attempting to determine the type and source of the explosive material and to examine the device and debris for trace evidence that can be linked to a suspect. Explosives in the criminal forensics context usually consist of improvised explosive materials or improvised explosive devices (IEDs) or both. Explosives can be made from almost any material that will burn, including gasoline, gunpowder, or even fertilizer. Explosive devices or containers can also be manufactured from readily available materials, such as a pipe bomb or even a pressure cooker. Explosive material and debris are chemically analyzed by forensic scientists to determine its nature and possible source. Explosion debris is carefully searched for trace evidence such as DNA or fingerprints.

DOI: 10.4324/9781041136361-16

13.1 UNDERSTANDING FIRE

It is important for fire investigators to understand what a fire is. A fire is the product of combustion, which is a chemical reaction between oxygen and a fuel. For the reaction to occur, the fuel must be heated to the point where it will react with the oxygen in the air. So the three elements of fire are known as the "fire triangle" – heat, fuel, and oxygen. A fuel can be any liquid, solid, or gas that gets heated to the point where it becomes a gas, and then it reacts with the oxygen to produce fire. To extinguish fire, one of the three elements must be removed. The heat can be removed by cooling, like placing water on the fire. The oxygen can be removed by smothering the flame, either physically or chemically with a fire extinguisher. The fuel can be physically removed, like when forest firefighters create a firebreak to prevent the fire from getting to more trees or brush.

In house fires, oxygen can be an important factor. In a closed room or building, the oxygen supply may dwindle, but if a window or door is opened or broken, the oxygen rushes in to feed the fire in what is called a "backdraft." Further, as objects in a room burn, the fire produces smoke and gases that collect at the ceiling. As the fire continues and the heat increases, those gases ultimately erupt in a violent flame known as "flashover." These phenomena are important not only because they pose serious dangers to the firefighters but also because they can destroy evidence that could be valuable in determining the origin and cause of the fire.

13.2 FIRE ORIGIN AND CAUSE INVESTIGATION

The primary use of forensic science evidence relating to fires is to attempt to identify the origin of the fire and to determine whether and what type of an accelerant was used to start or spread a fire. These investigations are critical to determining if the fire was accidental or intentionally set by arson.

Determining the origin of a fire is difficult because much of the evidence has usually been destroyed by the fire itself. Several myths about fire origin were prevalent among fire investigators and some persist. It was thought that fires burned in a "V" shape and that therefore the origin of the fire would be at the bottom of the V and can indicate arson. The theory was that any burning on the house floor indicated that the fire was intentionally set there. Scientific experiments have since proven that a "V" shape is often the result of flashover or other factors and unrelated to the original source of the fire (Gorbett, 2015).

Determining the cause of a fire is, of course, the crucial element in deciding whether it was arson. One critical factor is whether there was an accelerant. The presence of an accelerant is most often detected by its smell. Some agencies use dogs to direct an investigator to a location for further investigation. Others use commercially available electronic sniffers to detect areas for possible investigation, similar to devices that had been used to detect combustible gases in mines. Gasoline or other petroleum-based products, of course, are the dominant form of accelerants used in intentionally set fires. Cause determinations, especially for accelerants, proceed on a much stronger scientific footing. If an accelerant is detected, the task then is to attempt to individualize the particular accelerant. Fire debris is examined in the laboratory to identify common petroleum-based products. The industry standard is to use gas chromatography. Based on the results of the gas chromatography, petroleum products may be identified generally by classification, such as gasoline, according to a recognized petroleum distillate classification system.

Determining the cause of the fire, especially related to accelerants, has had its own myths. It was believed that gasoline, for example, burns at a higher temperature than wood, when the temperature of the burn is related to the amount of oxygen rather than the fuel. It was also thought that evidence of a "puddle" in the burn indicated a liquid accelerant, but the flashover effect can cause puddling burns. These false ideas were perpetuated as fire investigators passed down their lore to others. In 2009, the NAS Report expressed its findings and doubts about the validity of fire cause and origin testimony:

> [M]uch more research is needed on the natural variability of burn patterns and damage characteristics and how they are affected by the presence of various accelerants. Despite the paucity of research, some arson investigators continue to make determinations about whether or not a particular fire was set. However, according to testimony presented to the committee, many of the rules of thumb that are typically assumed to indicate that an accelerant was used . . . have been shown not to be true. Experiments should be designed to put arson investigations on a more solid scientific footing.
>
> National Research Council (2009) at p. 173

A significant issue in fire origin testimony is the lack of scientific qualifications of supposed experts, who are often local fire marshals. One of the foremost experts on fire origin, John Lentini, described the problem:

> [T]he majority of practitioners of this "scientific" endeavor are not scientists and have little, if any, scientific training education. . . . [I]t is difficult to argue thart individuals who have a limited understanding of the chemistry and physics of fire development can draw reasonable conclusions about fires. Yet, most practitioners do not possess a bachelor's degree. With the exception of fire debris chemists . . . the people who investigate fires and explosions acquired their experience one fire at a time, as firefighters, and later as fire investigators. . . . The skills required to extinguish a fire are quite different than those required to investigate a fire.
>
> Lentini (2013) at p. 247

As a result of scientific investigation and the discovery of wrongful convictions based on untrained fire marshal testimony, including the execution of an apparently innocent man (see the Willingham Case Study), much progress has been made toward making fire origin and cause investigation a more scientifically reliable forensic science.

In 2011, the National Fire Protection Association adopted NFPA 921, a Guide for Fire and Explosion Investigation. This standard is a crucial document setting forth the methodology for conducting accurate fire investigations. It has been revised and improved since 2011. Like its predecessors, the 2024 edition stresses a scientific method for conducting investigations and requires that investigators use a systematic and objective process (National Fire Protection Association, 2024). It includes the fundamentals of fire, including ignition and fire spread patterns, and depends on making empirical and measurable evidence without the traditional assumptions. NFPA 921 is considered the authoritative guide for fire investigators. It has had a significant impact on the fire investigation and standardized the methods and techniques used by most investigators today (Lentini, 2020).

13.3 EXPLOSIONS

The National Fire Protection Association defines an explosion as the "sudden conversion of potential energy (chemical or mechanical) into kinetic energy with the production and release of gases under pressure, or the release of gas under pressure." (National Fire Protection Association, 2024). Explosives in the criminal forensics context usually consist of explosive materials, IEDs, or both. The primary purposes of the forensic investigation of explosions and explosive devices are to determine the type and source of the explosive material and to retrieve any trace evidence from the device or debris that can be linked to a suspect.

Explosives can be made from almost any material that will burn, including gasoline, gunpowder, or even fertilizer. Residue from the explosive will often be left after the explosion. To locate the residue investigators may use a handheld chemical detection device. The residue will then be examined by a forensic chemist, using gas chromatography, mass spectrometry, x-ray analysis, and other available techniques. The federal Bureau of Alcohol, Tobacco, Firearms and Explosives (ATF) operates the U.S. Bomb Data Center which has a database of National maintains a database of explosive materials (Bureau of Alcohol, Tobacco, Firearms & Explosives, 2019). The ATF may also be able to trace a particular explosive material to a manufacturer and possibly a purchaser.

Explosive devices range from manufactured bombs, grenades, mines, sticks of dynamite, or even fireworks. But explosive devices or containers can also be improvised from readily available materials, such as a pipe bomb or even a pressure cooker. The FBI operates the Terrorist Explosive Device Analytical Center (TEDAC) as a database of IEDs (Federal Bureau of Investigation, n.d.).

A very important part of forensic explosion investigation is the collection of debris from the explosive device. The explosion will leave pieces of the container and perhaps any of the shrapnel or other contents of the device at the crime scene. Explosion debris can then be carefully searched for trace evidence, such as DNA or fingerprints, that can lead to the suspect.

CASE STUDY The Cameron Todd Willingham Execution

Cameron Todd Willingham was executed in Texas for the alleged murder of his three children by setting fire to his own home where the children were sleeping. He was convicted based on testimony from a Texas fire marshal investigator that the fire in Willingham's home had burned "fast and hot" and had been started using a liquid accelerant. The fire marshal relied on his observations that there were char patterns in the floor in the shape of "puddles," multiple starting points of the fire, "crazed glass" damage, and a positive test for "mineral spirits," all indicating to him that the fire had been ignited with the help of a liquid accelerant. He also testified that Willingham's statement that he had run out of the house to avoid the fire was not believable because he did not have burns consistent with that story (Figure 13.1).

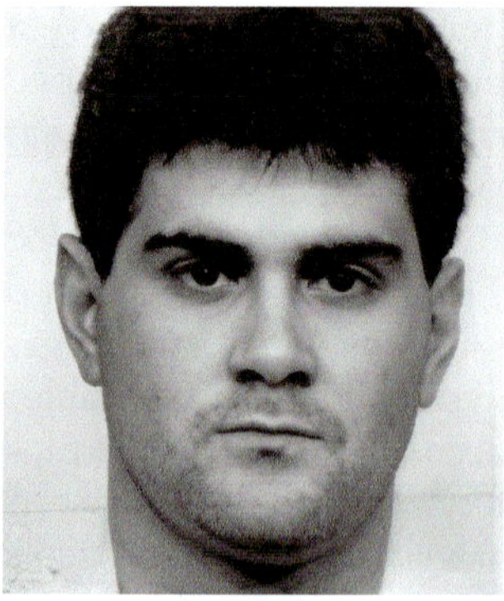

Figure 13.1 Cameron Todd Willingham

Source: Getty

On appeal, the Texas Court of Criminal Appeals summarized the fire origin expert testimony in simple terms:

> An expert witness for the State testified that the floors, front threshold, and front concrete porch were burned, which only occurs when an accelerant has been used to purposely burn these areas. This witness further testified that this igniting of the floors and thresholds is typically employed to impede firemen in their rescue attempts.

Willingham's habeas corpus petition to the federal court was denied and his last petition for certiorari to the U.S. Supreme Court was denied on November 3, 2003.

Prior to Willingham's execution, Gerald Hurst, a fire origin expert working *pro bono* for the defense made a detailed report finding that the conclusions of arson made by the fire investigators were invalid and stated:

> The Fire Investigation Report of the Texas State Fire Marshal's office in this case is a remarkable document. On first reading, a contemporary fire origin and cause analyst might well wonder how anyone could make so many critical errors. However when the report is looked at in the context of its time and in light of a few key advances that have been made in the fire investigation field in the last dozen years, it becomes obvious that the report more or less simply reflects the shortcomings in the state of the art prior to the beginning of serious efforts to introduce standards and to test old theories that had previously been accepted on faith. . . . As will be shown later, most of the conclusions reached by the Fire Marshal would be considered invalid in light of current knowledge.

The report was sent to the Texas Board of Pardons and Paroles and to Texas Governor Rick Perry. The Board voted unanimously to recommend the denial of clemency, which the Governor did, and Willingham was executed on February 17, 2004.

Willingham's execution in spite of the Hurst report quickly generated press coverage detailing the controversy over the validity of the fire origin expert testimony in his case, including a statement by Hurst that "[t]here's nothing to suggest to any reasonable arson investigator that this was an arson fire." Three other experts also reached a similar conclusion. In 2006, the Innocence Project asked the newly formed Texas Forensic Science Commission to review the Willingham case and another case. The Commission eventually commissioned its own review by another reputable fire origin expert, Dr. Craig Beyler. In his August 2009 report, Beyler concluded:

> The investigations of the Willis and Willingham fires did not comport with either the modern standard of care expressed by NFPA 921, or the standard of care expressed by fire investigation texts and papers in the period 1980–1992. The investigators had poor understandings of fire science and failed to acknowledge or apply the contemporaneous understanding of the limitations of fire indicators. Their methodologies did not comport with the scientific method or the process of elimination. A finding of arson could not be sustained based upon the standard of care expressed by NFPA 921, or the standard of care expressed by fire investigation texts and papers in the period 1980–1992.

Of the Fire Marshal who testified in Willingham's case, Beyler was extremely critical:

> His statistics of the fraction of fires which are in fact arson are remarkable and far exceed any rational estimate. It reflects his predisposition to find arson in his cases. This directly violates NFPA 921 and professional norms in general. His quotations that "The fire tells a story, I am just the interpreter," and "the fire does not lie, it tells me the truth," are hardly consistent with a scientific mindset and is more characteristic of mystics or psychics. The quotes separate the findings from his own judgment and seek to make him not responsible for his own interpretation. It seems to deny the role of rational reasoning. It is an expression of fire investigation as a mystical art rather than an application of science and reason.

A lengthy media report brought further national attention to the case, and a political firestorm ensued. Prosecutors and politicians reacted strongly against the Beyler report, and just days before Beyler was to present his findings to the Commission, Governor Perry replaced four of its members with new appointees, including naming a vocal opponent of the report as the chair. The political maneuvering to prevent an official report that Willingham was wrongfully executed intensified with the announced candidacy of Governor Perry for President. A "final" report of the Commission was eventually issued on April 15, 2011, in which the Commission critically reviewed the Willingham evidence and recommended a series of education and training improvements for fire investigators. It did not make any findings regarding the conduct of the fire investigators in the case because it claimed it had no jurisdiction to do so. On July 29, 2011, the Texas Attorney General issued an opinion restricting the Commission's jurisdiction and the Commission then issued a "Final Report Addendum" in which it adopted the Attorney General's restricted view of the Commission's jurisdiction and effectively ended the investigation.

The Willingham case resulted in some major media reporting as well as a documentary film and even a major motion picture (Grann, 2009; *Incendiary: The Willingham Case*, 2011; *Trial By Fire*, 2018).

CASE STUDY The Boston Marathon Bombing

On April 15, 2013, two terrorist brothers planted two bombs that detonated near the finish line of the Boston Marathon race, killing three people and injuring hundreds of others. The two bombs were homemade from pressure cookers. The cookers were filled with gunpowder, nails, and ball bearings to act as shrapnel and intensify the human damage. The gunpowder was from fireworks one of the brothers had purchased and stripped. The men placed the bombs inside backpacks in the crowd and detonated them using a remote device. One of the bombers later said that he learned how to make the bombs from a magazine (Figure 13.2).

Based on video from the scene and eyewitness statements, the FBI identified the brothers. After a large manhunt in which the brothers shot and killed a local police officer and kidnapped and hijacked a civilian, there was a shootout where they detonated another pressure-cooker bomb and threw several homemade grenades. One of the brothers was killed at that scene and the other injured brother, Dzhokhar, was eventually captured after hiding in a boat behind a residence in the area. On June 24, 2015, then 22-year-old Dzhokhar Tsarnaev was sentenced to death after being convicted of 30 criminal charges. As of 2025, he is still being held on death row (Federal Bureau of Investigation, *Boston Marathon Bombing*, n.d.).

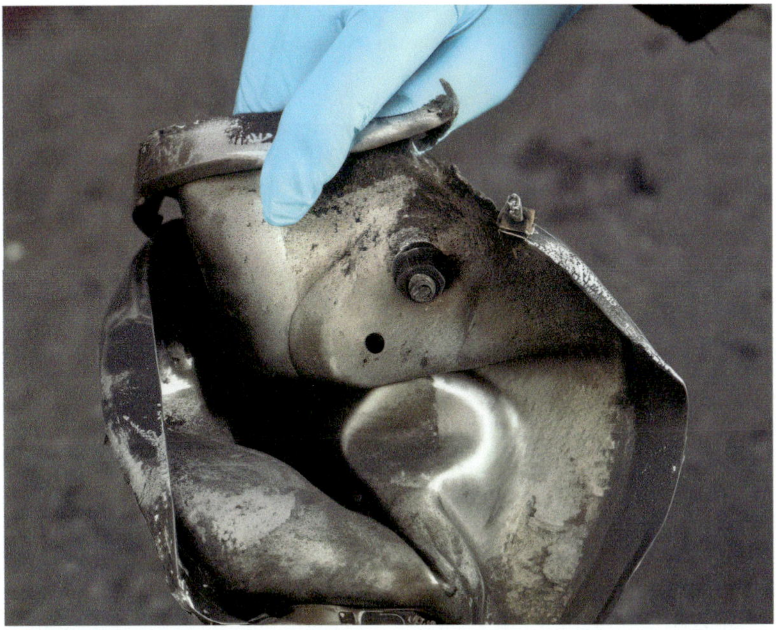

Figure 13.2 Portion of the Pressure Cooker Bomb Recovered from the Boston Marathon Bombing.

Source: FBI

REFERENCES

Bureau of Alcohol, Tobacco, Firearms & Explosives, *About the U.S. Bomb Data Center*, U.S. Department of Homeland Security (2019) https://www.atf.gov/explosives/about-us-bomb-data-center

Federal Bureau of Investigation, *Boston Marathon Bombing*, U.S. Department of Justice (n.d.) https://www.fbi.gov/history/famous-cases/boston-marathon-bombing

Federal Bureau of Investigation, *Terrorist Explosive Device Analytical Center (TEDAC)*, U.S Department of Justice (n.d.) https://www.fbi.gov/investigate/terrorism/tedac

Gorbett, G., et al., *Use of Damage in Fire Investigation: A Review of Fire Patterns Analysis, Research and Future Direction*, 4 Fire Sci. Rev. 4 (2015) https://doi.org/10.1186/s40038-015-0008-4

Grann, D., *Trial by Fire*, New Yorker Magazine (August 31, 2009) https://www.newyorker.com/magazine/2009/09/07/trial-by-fire?yrail=

Incendiary: The Willingham Case (2011) https://www.imdb.com/title/tt1744847/

Lentini, J., *Fire, Arsons and Explosions*, chapter 39 in *Modern Scientific Evidence*, 2013–2014 ed., Faigman, D., Kaye, D., Saks, M., and Sanders, J. (Eds.) (2013). Thomson Reuters.

Lentini, J., *A Model for Confronting Fire Investigation Errors*, 7 Lincoln Mem'l U. L. Rev. 1 (2020) https://digitalcommons.lmunet.edu/lmulrev/vol7/iss2/1

National Fire Protection Association, *NFPA 921 Guide for Fire and Explosion Investigations* (2024) https://www.nfpa.org/en/codes-and-standards/nfpa-921-standard-development/921

National Research Council of the National Academies of Science, *Analysis of Hair Evidence, Strengthening Forensic Science in the United States: A Path Forward* (2009) https://nap.nationalacademies.org/catalog/12589/strengthening-forensic-science-in-the-united-states-a-path-forward

Trial by Fire (2018) https://www.imdb.com/title/tt3263946/

READINGS

AAAS, *Forensic Science Assessments: A Quality and Gap Analysis-Fire Investigation* (Report July 11, 2017) https://www.aaas.org/resources/fire-investigation

American Association for the Advancement of Science, *Forensic Science Assessments: A Quality and Gap Analysis-Fire Investigation.*, National Commission on Forensic Science (Dec. 8, 2015). https://www.justice.gov/ncfs/file/798986/dl?inline=

American Association for the Advancement of Science (AAAS) (2017) https://www.academia.edu/38765450/Fire_Investigation_A_Quality_and_Gap_Analysis

Beety, V. and Oliva, J., *Evidence on Fire*, 97 N. C. L. Rev. 483 (2019) https://scholarship.law.unc.edu/nclr/vol97/iss3/1/

Dioso-Villa, R., *Scientific and Legal Developments in Fire and Arson Investigation Expertise in Texas v. Willingham*, 14 Minn. J. L. Sci. Tech. 817 (2013) https://scholarship.law.umn.edu/mjlst/vol14/iss2/8/

FEMA, *Fire Investigation: First Responders Student Manual*, U.S. Department of Homeland Security (2025) https://apps.usfa.fema.gov/ax/sm/sm_0770.pdf

Lentini, J., *Fire Investigation: Historical Perspective and Recent Developments*, 31 Forensic Sci. Rev. 37 (2019) https://www.academia.edu/38765447/Fire_Investigation_Historical_Perspective_and_Recent_Developments

Lentini, J., *Fire Scene Inspection Methodology and Collection of Evidence*, chapter in *Encyclopedia of Forensic Sciences* (3d ed., 2022) https://www.sciencedirect.com/science/article/abs/pii/B9780128236772002415?via%3Dihub

McKelvey, T., *Forensics Investigators Decode the Boston Bombings*, BBC News (April 17, 2013) https://www.bbc.com/news/world-us-canada-22178280

National Institute of Justice, *A Guide for Investigating Fire and Arson*, U.S. Department of Justice (2009) https://nij.ojp.gov/topics/articles/guide-investigating-fire-and-arson

14

Bloodstains and Patterns

14.1 BLOODSTAINS

Investigators often view, record, and collect blood from a crime scene. The preliminary question sometimes is whether the particular substance is indeed a human bloodstain or some other substance. The presence or absence of blood can be an important piece of evidence. Investigators may want to make presumptive tests to see if a stain may be blood at the scene. Several chemicals may be used to make such field determinations, the most common of which is luminol. Criminal investigators use the same reaction to detect traces of blood at crime scenes. Luminol powder is mixed with hydrogen peroxide and a hydroxide. When the solution is sprayed on blood, the iron from the hemoglobin in the blood acts as a catalyst for the reaction that produces a blue glow. Unfortunately, luminol is known to produce false positives, indicating that the stain is blood when it is some other substance (Barni, 2007). Other presumptive tests include the Kastle-Meyer test where a swab of the substance is placed in a test tube with phenolphthalein and then hydrogen peroxide to see if the reaction turns pink indicating that hemoglobin is present. It can also return false positives (Glaister, 1926). Ultimately, to be admissible, a laboratory confirmatory test is required. The most common of the confirmatory tests are known as the Takayama test and the Teichmann test, and they are fairly simple chemical procedures (National Institute of Justice, 2023). A laboratory precipitin test can confirm whether the blood is from a human (Figure 14.1).

DOI: 10.4324/9781041136361-17

14.2 BLOOD PATTERN ANALYSIS

Figure 14.1 Blood Pattern Analysis.

Source: Shutterstock

The important forensic question is what conclusions can be drawn from a pattern of bloodstains or spattering. Acts of violence, from a gunshot, knife, or other weapon, can cause a dispersion of blood along a trajectory from the wound. The blood droplets usually emerge in a spherical shape and can end up on a surface like a wall, ceiling, or floor. Blood pattern analysis (BPA) is the process of drawing conclusions from the patterns on those surfaces. It is used to form the basis for testimony about such issues as the sequence of events, the distance from which a victim was shot, claims of self-defense, and any number of other homicide or assault dynamics. It may include the determination of whether a stain resulted from arterial spurting, blood dripping, aspirated (coughed) blood, back spatter, angular deposits, flight paths, or many other characteristics of the blood path that led to the recorded bloodstain pattern.

The analysis of bloodstain patterns is based on a complex application of the principles of biology, chemistry, and physics, especially fluid dynamics. "A detailed understanding of blood dynamics and stain formation is an essential prerequisite to the interpretation of both individual bloodstains and spatter patterns." Adam (2012) at p.77.

BPA focuses on the analysis of the size, shape, and distribution of bloodstains resulting from bloodshed events as a means of determining the types of activities and mechanisms that produced them. . . . BPA is a discipline that uses the fields of biology, physics, and mathematics.

James, (2005)

The NAS Report summarized its highly critical assessment regarding bloodstain pattern analysis:

> Scientific studies support some aspects of bloodstain pattern analysis. One can tell, for example, if the blood spattered quickly or slowly, but some experts extrapolate far beyond what can be supported. Although the trajectories of bullets are linear, the damage that they cause in soft tissue and the complex patterns that fluids make when exiting wounds are highly variable. For such situations, many experiments must be conducted to determine what characteristics of a bloodstain pattern are caused by particular actions during a crime and to inform the interpretation of those causal links and their variabilities. For these same reasons, extra care must be given to the way in which the analyses are presented

> in court. The uncertainties associated with bloodstain pattern analysis are enormous.
>
> National Research Council (2009) at pp. 178–179.

A major problem with BPA is the lack of qualifications of persons who have been allowed to testify about bloodstain pattern conclusions. Notwithstanding the claimed basis of the practice in biology and physics, there are no formal educational requirements for people who claim to be experts in BPA. Some professional organizations, such as the International Association for Identification (IAI) and the Scientific Working Group on Bloodstain Pattern Analysis (SWGSTAIN), recommend training and workshops, but those requirements are minimal (International Association for Identification, 2025; Scientific Working Group on Bloodstain Pattern Analysis, 2008).

Unfortunately, much bloodstain pattern testimony is often offered by police officers based on little education in fluid dynamics and limited hard evidence. For example, in State v. Hust, NM Supreme Court (2024), a police detective testified as a bloodstain pattern expert in a rape and murder case and the New Mexico Supreme Court said, "Any perceived deficiencies in Detective Brown's education and training are relevant to the weight the jury accords to an expert's testimony, not to the testimony's admissibility." The legal history of bloodstain pattern testimony from such experts has been characterized by almost routine acceptance of qualifications and findings of admissibility. Courts are willing to qualify experts on minimal credentials, even after *Daubert*. In *State v. Davolt*, the Arizona Supreme Court approved the trial court's qualification of a police detective as an expert bloodstain pattern analyst in a death penalty case because:

> Detective Harry's training in blood splatter analysis consisted of attending classes on crime scene management, a class on homicide investigation, and watching two training videos on blood splatter analysis as part of his advanced officer training at the Lake Havasu Police Department. While this training is not extensive, it is significantly more extensive than the average person has received and is sufficient to allow the testimony to be heard by the jury. *State v. Davolt*, 207 Ariz. 191, 84 P.3d 456 (2004) at p. 485.

REFERENCES

Adam, C., *Fundamental Studies of Bloodstain Formation and Characteristics*, 219(1–3) Forensic Sci Int. 76–87 (June 10, 2012) https://doi.org/10.1016/j.forsciint.2011.12.002

Barni, F., et al., *Forensic Application of the Luminol Reaction as a Presumptive Test for Latent Blood Detection*, 72 Talanta 3 (2007) https://www.sciencedirect.com/science/article/pii/S0039914007000082

Glaister, J., *The Kastle-Meyer Test for the Detection of Blood: Considered from the Medico-Legal Aspect*, 10 Br. Med. J. 1 (1926) https://pmc.ncbi.nlm.nih.gov/articles/PMC2523691/

International Association for Identification, *Bloodstain Pattern Analyst Certification* (2025) https://www.theiai.org/bloodstain_pattern.php

James, S., et al., *Principles of Bloodstain Pattern Analysis: Theory and Practice* (2005). CRC Press.

National Institute of Justice, *Laboratory Orientation and Testing of Body Fluids and Tissues for Forensic Analysts* (2023) https://nij.ojp.gov/nij-hosted-online-training-courses/laboratory-orientation-and-testing-body-fluids-and-tissues/testing-body-fluids-tissues/blood/confirmatory-tests

National Research Council of the National Academies of Science, *Analysis of Hair Evidence, Strengthening Forensic Science in the United States: A Path Forward* (2009) https://nap.nationalacademies.org/catalog/12589/strengthening-forensic-science-in-the-united-states-a-path-forward

Scientific Working Group on Bloodstain Pattern Analysis (SWGSTAIN), *Guidelines for the Minimum Educational and Training Requirements for Bloodstain Pattern Analysts*, U.S. Department of Justice (2008) https://www.ojp.gov/ncjrs/virtual-library/abstracts/scientific-working-group-bloodstain-pattern-analysis-guidelines

State v. Davolt, 207 Ariz. 191, 84 P.3d 456 (2004).

State v. Hust, *NM Supreme Court*, No. S-1-SC-39555 (2024) https://law.justia.com/cases/new-mexico/supreme-court/2024/s-1-sc-39555.html

READINGS

Fischer, W., *Defining the "Address" of Bloodstains and Other Evidence at the Crime Scene*, chapter in *Scientific and Legal Applications of Bloodstain Pattern Analysis*, James, Stuart H. (ed.) (1991). CRC Press.

Virkler, K. and Lednev, I., *Analysis of Body Fluids for Forensic Purposes: From Laboratory Testing to Non-Destructive Rapid Confirmatory Identification at a Crime Scene*, 188 Forensic Sci. Int. 1–3 (2009) https://www.sciencedirect.com/science/article/pii/S0379073809000826

Wonder, A., *Blood Dynamics* (2001). Academic Press.

15

Gunshot Residue

During a shooting, the firing pin strikes the back of the cartridge, which then causes the primer to ignite the gunpowder and that explosion sends the bullet down the chamber. The metals in the primer material get vaporized, and those gases come out of the weapon, primarily the muzzle and breech area. These gases then quickly condense, and the metallic particles are left on anything close, including the hands of the shooter (Figure 15.1).

Gunshot residue does not last long and can be easily removed or rubbed away by many activities of the hands and can be easily wiped away. Hand washing will remove most of the particles. The particles can also be transferred from one person to another. Residue may also land on non-shooters within a couple of feet of the firing. Obviously, handguns are more likely to leave residue on the hands than rifles.

The residue is usually latent, and their identification requires the removal and preservation of samples that can be examined in the forensic laboratory. Investigators traditionally swabbed the hands of a suspect or took clothing for further examination. More recently gunshot residue kits provide an adhesive stub that is pressed against the hand to "lift" any particles for examination. For clothing, the same type of adhesive lifter is used, and residue on clothing usually lasts longer than on the hands.

15.1 RESIDUE ANALYSIS

Today, most gunshot residue analysis is conducted using spectrometric instruments. Most forensic laboratories use Scanning Electron Microscopy

DOI: 10.4324/9781041136361-18

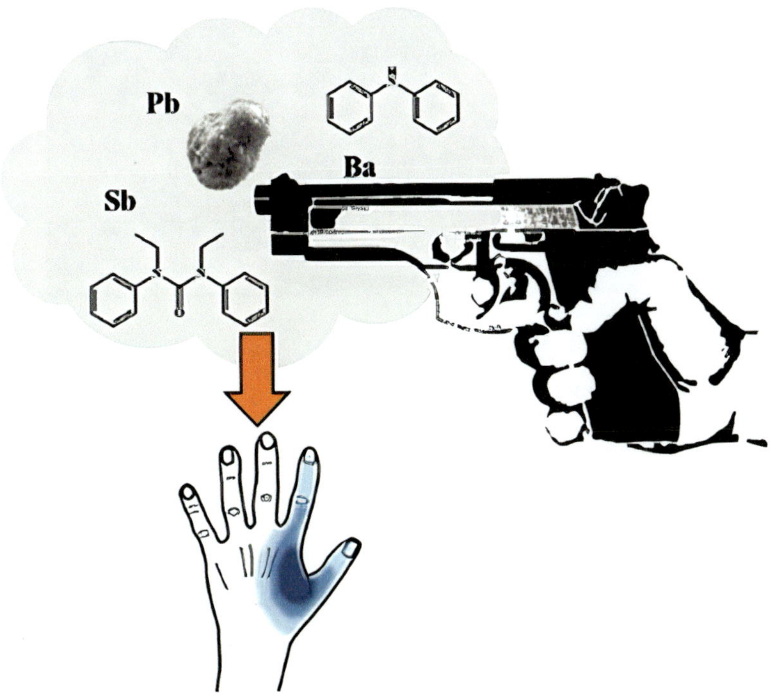

Figure 15.1 Gunshot Residue.

Source: Feeney, et al. https://www.sciencedirect.com/science/article/abs/pii/S2468170920300382

coupled with Energy Dispersive X-Ray Spectrometry, known as scanning electron microscopy coupled with energy dispersive X-Ray spectrometry (SEM-EDS) (Harshey, 2021). These tests are designed to disclose which chemicals are contained in the samples, in what quantities, and whether those chemicals are associated with gunpowder. The most common gunshot residue contains lead (Pb), barium (Ba), and antimony (Sb). Most cartridge primers contain the explosive lead styphnate (Pb), an oxidizing agent of barium nitrate (Ba), and antimony sulfide (Sb) as a fuel. If all three are identified, it can be a significant indication of gunshot residue (Dalby, 2010).

As the SEM-EDS instruments detect suspected gunshot chemical residue particles, the computer records the location and size of each particle. The analyst then reports the location and quantities of the residue particles

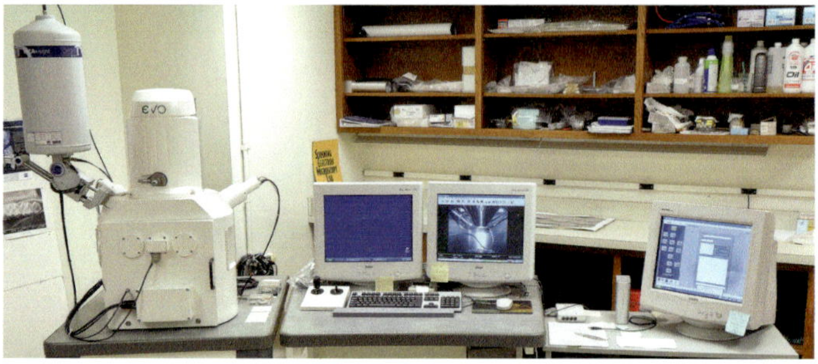

Figure 15.2 SEM-EDS Analysis.

Source: Field Museum

and purports to make a conclusion that the sample contains residue from a fired gun (Figure 15.2).

15.2 ADMISSIBILITY ISSUES

While most gunshot residue analysts have been permitted to testify, both before and after *Daubert*, there are issues concerning such testimony. The presence of lead, barium, and antimony chemical particles together is not unique to firearms. Fireworks, welding, and brake materials can also leave the same traces. Also, some types of primers do not contain one or more of those elements. The *Daubert* criterion relating to the presence of standards also poses an issue for gunshot residue testimony. There is no currently agreed standard for the number of particles that must be found before it can be said to be gunshot residue. Most forensic laboratories do not use a scientifically established threshold for reporting gunshot residue results and will report even one particle containing the chemical elements as being generated from a gunshot with a caveat that they are reporting a raw number. More recently, however, experts have concentrated on developing probabilistic likelihood ratios to relate the residue components to gunshot origins (Israelsohn, 2022).

Finally, a primary limitation on gunshot residue testimony is that while analysts can say that the particles came from a fired weapon, they cannot describe how or when they were deposited. One of the main issues with gunshot residue testing is cross-contamination. In 2006, the FBI stated that while it supported the science of GSR, the FBI would no longer conduct GSR testing (Bykowicz, May 28, 2006).

REFERENCES

Bykowicz, J., *FBI Ends Analysis of Gunshot Residue*, Baltimore Sun (May 28, 2006) https://www.chron.com/news/nation-world/article/fbi-ends-analysis-of-gunshot-residue-1655046.php

Dalby, O., et al., *Analysis of Gunshot Residue and Associated Materials – a Review*, 55 J. For. Sci. 4 (2010) https://onlinelibrary.wiley.com/toc/15564029/2010/55/4

Harshey, A., et al., *Trends in Gunshot Residue Detection by Electrochemical Methods for Forensic Purpose*, 5 J. Anal. Test. 258 (2021) https://doi.org/10.1007/s41664-020-00152-x

Israelsohn, A., et al, *A Likelihood-Ratio Framework for Evaluating Results of Forensic Gunshot-Residue Analysis*, 336 For. Sci. Intl. (2022) https://www.sciencedirect.com/science/article/pii/S0379073822001694

READINGS

Bykowicz, J., *In Priority Shift, FBI Halts Gunshot Residue Analysis*, Los Angeles Times (May 28, 2006) https://www.latimes.com/archives/la-xpm-2006-may-28-na-fbi28-story.html

Charles, S., Geusens, N. and Nys, B., *Interpol Review of Gunshot Residue 2019 to 2021*, 6 Forensic Sci. Int. Synerg. (2023) https://www.sciencedirect.com/science/article/pii/S2589871X22000870

Cioccia, G., et al., *Probabilistic-based Identification of Gunshot Residues (GSR) using Laser-Induced Breakdown Spectroscopy (LIBS) and Support Vector Machine (SVM) Algorithm*, 27 Microchem. J. (2024) https://www.sciencedirect.com/science/article/pii/S0026265X24022549

Dalby, O., et al., *Analysis of Gunshot Residue and Associated Materials – a Review*, 55 J. For. Sci. 4 (2010) https://onlinelibrary.wiley.com/toc/15564029/2010/55/4

McCutcheon, M., *Testing for Gun Shot Residue GSR Forensic Education*, YouTube, https://www.youtube.com/watch?v=6scYmo95hHI

Organization of Scientific Area Committees for Forensic Science (OSAC), *Standard Practice for the Collection and Preservation of Organic Gunshot Residue*, National Institute of Standards and Technology (NIST) (2021) https://www.nist.gov/system/files/documents/2021/02/01/Standard%20Practice%20for%20the%20Collection%20and%20Preservation%20of%20oGSR_DRAFT%20OSAC%20PROPOSED.pdf

Penven, D., *Gun Shot Residue Testing: Is It Still a Viable Form of Physical Evidence?* Crime Scene Investigator Network (2013) https://www.crime-scene-investigator.net/gsrstillviable.html

Romolo, F. and Margot, P., *Identification of Gunshot Residue: A Critical Review*, 119 Forensic Sci. Int. 2 (2001) https://www.sciencedirect.com/science/article/pii/S037907380000428X

Serol, M., Ahmad, S., Quintas, A. and Família, C., *Chemical Analysis of Gunpowder and Gunshot Residues*, 20 Molecules 28 (2023) https://pmc.ncbi.nlm.nih.gov/articles/PMC10386329/

16

Medical Examiner Testimony

There are two primary issues regarding the admissibility of the testimony of a medical examiner or "coroner." The first is the qualifications of the supposed expert, and the second is testimony about the "manner of death."

16.1 CORONERS AND MEDICAL EXAMINERS

The history of the position of coroner goes back centuries to England. Both homicide and suicide were crimes, and the king was entitled to all the possessions of the murderer or the person who committed suicide. A coroner was appointed by the government to determine whether it was homicide or suicide, primarily to make sure that the crown got its money. There were also death taxes that the coroner was required to collect. The coroner position was later adopted in colonial America as a means of investigating how a death occurred. The coroner was not a doctor and there was no science involved in the investigations. The coroner, often using a jury of local folks, would decide if the decedent had been murdered and, if so, notify the local sheriff. In many States, the position of coroner has persisted as an elected or appointed position with little or no requirements for any medical expertise.

On the other hand, many jurisdictions use a medical examiner to examine the body and certify the cause and manner of death for public health purposes. Beginning in the late 1800s, some States replaced the coroner system with a requirement for a medically trained person, known as a medical examiner. The federal government defines a medical examiner as a "forensic pathologist whose duty is to oversee medicolegal

DOI: 10.4324/9781041136361-19

death investigations, perform postmortem examinations, and certify cause and manner of death." National Institute of Standards and Technology (2025). However, even some of the States that use a medical examiner system do not necessarily require that the doctor be a pathologist or forensic pathologist. Indeed, the definition of a "medical examiner" varies among jurisdictions. Some States have a centralized medical examiner system, but most have medical examiners who are appointed locally (Haazlick, 2003).

Medical examiners and coroners investigate sudden or unexpected deaths, deaths without an attending physician, or any suspicious and violent death. The medicolegal system is very diverse. According to the Justice Department in 2018, 34 states had city, county, district, or regional medicolegal death investigation systems: 13 had coroner systems; 7 had medical examiner systems; and 14 had both coroners and medical examiner systems. At that time, there were still 2,210 non-physician coroners in the country, mostly in smaller jurisdictions (Bureau of Justice Statistics, 2018). In 2015, the National Commission on Forensic Science (NCFS) called for accreditation of medical examiners and coroners offices and for certification of medicolegal death investigators. (National Commission on Forensic Science, 2015). Medical examiners can be certified by the National Association of Medical Examiners (NAME), or the International Association of Coroners and Medical Examiners (IACME), or the American Board of Independent Medical Examiners. But by 2018, only 17% of the medical examiner or coroner offices were accredited by any of these organizations (Bureau of Justice Statistics, 2018).

NATIONAL ACADEMY OF SCIENCES REPORT (2009)

ME/C systems function at varying levels of expertise, often with deficiencies in facilities, equipment, staff, education, and training. And, unfortunately, most systems are under budgeted and understaffed. As with other forensic science fields, there are no mandated national qualifications or certifications required for death investigators. Nor is medical expertise always required. In addition, there is no one recognized set of performance standards or best practices for ME/C systems nor are there incentives to implement one recognized set. Also lacking are universally accepted or promulgated methods of quality control or quality assurance.

National Research Council (2009) at pp. 264–265.

16.2 THE ADMISSIBILITY OF "MANNER OF DEATH" OPINIONS

Medical examiners and even coroners are often routinely allowed to testify about both the "cause" and "manner" of death. See, e.g., Sippio v. State, 350 Md. 633, 714 A.2d 864 (1998)

"Cause" is the medical reason for death, such as a heart attack, loss of blood, or asphyxiation. These are medical findings made by a physician. "Manner," however, is a conclusion about how the medical condition came about and whether it resulted from natural causes, an accident, suicide, or homicide. Medical examiners are statutorily required to make those findings administratively to make an entry on a death certificate, which is used for public health purposes. But the manner of death conclusion is not necessarily drawn from any medical findings but rather depends on evidence of other ordinary circumstances, usually provided by the police or by the medical examiner's observations at the scene. For purposes of a criminal trial, there is a significant question about whether medical examiners should be able to testify to such a legal conclusion (Figure 16.1).

Courts are divided about admitting manner of death conclusions by doctors. Courts always permit medical examiners to testify about the cause of death because that is a medical opinion, usually based on the results of an autopsy. It is clearly within the expertise of a physician. Some courts admit both cause and manner testimony in almost every case, but some courts have excluded or limited manner of death testimony from doctors, when the testimony was based primarily on nonmedical evidence. The

Figure 16.1 Mixing Medicine and Law.

Source: Quizlet.com

most notable of such cases is State v. Tyler, 867 N.W.2d 136 (Iowa 2015), which is discussed below.

Daubert and Rule 702, especially as recently amended, require the judge to first ensure that the witness has the expertise, based on knowledge, skill, experience, training, or education, to offer an expert opinion in his or her area. Doctors are certainly qualified to offer opinions as to the medical cause of death. However, determining the manner of death – how it happened – is an interpretation of nonmedical, ordinary facts and circumstances that have nothing to do with medical training or expertise. The jury must decide whether there was a homicide, for example, by listening to or observing the evidence that is offered in open court under oath. Allowing a doctor to decide the manner of death invades the jury function. And the jury is well qualified to make that conclusion based on sworn testimony, cross-examination, and the rules of evidence and procedure.

Further, *Daubert* requires that all expert opinion be demonstrably reliable based on the factors of testing, error rate, standards, peer review, and general acceptance. The opinion of a doctor about whether a murder was committed is not a science, it is a conclusion based on facts that have nothing to do with medicine. Such an opinion could never be tested scientifically. It would never have an error rate. And there are certainly no standards for making such a conclusion. The standard for a jury is proof beyond a reasonable doubt, and that is not within the province of a medical examiner. Legal scholars have called for an end to allowing medical examiners or coroners to testify as to the manner of death (Epstein, 2025; Findley, 2022; Kukucka, 2024).

CASE STUDY State v. Tyler, 867 N.W.2d 136, 162 (Iowa 2015)

Hillary Tyler delivered a fetus alone in a rented motel room. After she left, staff found blood in the room and the police were called. The police found the baby's body in a wastebasket. Tyler was arrested and, without giving her *Miranda* rights, she was questioned in the car on the way to the station and then for three hours at the station. She said that the baby was stillborn, did not move, and was placed in the wastebasket. According to the interrogators, she later changed her story and said that the baby had cried and moved, and that she drowned him in the bathtub. Eventually Tyler was taken to the hospital, where she was treated for preeclampsia and blood loss and received a surgical repair for a tear from childbirth. She was charged with first-degree murder. At her trial, she claimed that her statements to the police were coerced and not credible (Figure 16.2).

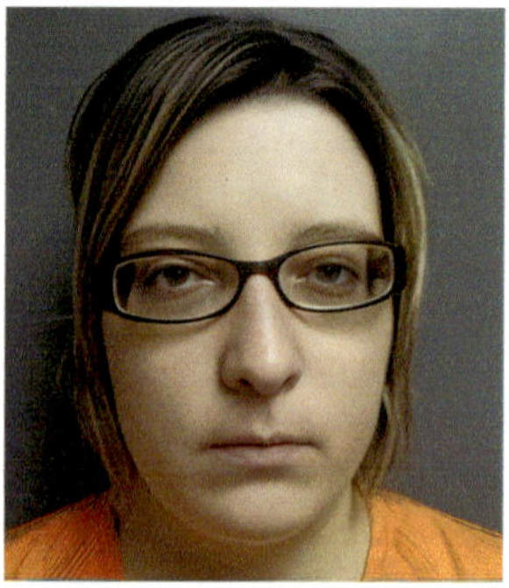

Figure 16.2 Hillary Tyler.

After an autopsy on the fetus, the medical examiner stated that the cause and manner of death were "undetermined." The police then gave him the police reports and provided him with video and audio recordings of Tyler's statements to the police. He then made a final report stating that the cause of death was as "Bathtub drowning" and the manner of death was "Homicide."

The defense moved to exclude his testimony. During a hearing, the forensic pathologist was questioned:

Q. *In this case, if you based your opinions speaking strictly on medical or scientific evidence, you were unable to give a conclusion as to whether or not this was a homicide, correct?*
A. *Just on the autopsy findings, that would be correct, yes.*
Q. *Okay. And also based just on the autopsy findings, you would be unable to determine whether or not this was a drowning, correct?*
A. *That would be correct, yes.*
Q. *The autopsy findings were consistent with intrauterine fetal demise [still birth], correct?*
A. *They could be, yes.*
Q. *They could also be consistent with a baby that died immediately after birth, correct?*
A. *It could be, yes.*

. . .

Q. *Okay. So the specific autopsy, the testing that you did, the toxicology test, the examination of the lungs, all of the things you did, the examination of the stomach contents, all of that led you to an inconclusive determination, correct?*

A. That's correct, yes.
Q. And the only way that you reached the conclusion of homicide as the manner of death, as drowning as a cause of death, is through observing and watching the videotapes that the law enforcement officers supplied to you, correct?
A. Yes, it is.

The judge nevertheless allowed the pathologist to testify as to both cause and manner of death, and Tyler was convicted of second-degree murder.

On appeal, the Iowa Supreme Court reversed the conviction and held that the trial court abused its discretion in allowing the medical examiner to testify to the cause and manner of Baby Tyler's death because the medical examiner based his opinions primarily, if not exclusively, on Tyler's inconsistent and uncorroborated statements to the police as opposed to objective, scientific, or medical evidence. The Court said, "[W]hen a medical examiner over-relies on witness statements or information obtained through police investigation in forming his or her opinions on cause or manner of death, such opinions may not assist the trier of fact" and further said that such opinions are not admissible because they "are not sufficiently based on scientific, technical, or specialized knowledge."

The Iowa Supreme Court ordered a new trial without the medical examiner testimony. On the eve of the retrial, Tyler pled guilty to reduced charges of child endangerment causing serious injury, first-degree criminal mischief, and abuse of a corpse. She was sentenced to 20 years in prison in 2017.

REFERENCES

Bureau of Justice Statistics, Office of Justice Programs, *Medical Examiner and Coroner Offices, 2018*, U.S. Department of Justice (2021) https://bjs.ojp.gov/content/pub/pdf/meco18.pdf

Epstein, J., *Is "Manner of Death" More or Less "Science" Than "Cause of Death?"*, American Bar Association Criminal Justice Magazine (July 18, 2025) https://www.americanbar.org/groups/criminal_justice/resources/magazine/2025-summer/manner-death-more-or-less-science-cause-death/

Findley, K. and Strang, D., *Ending Manner of Death Testimony and Other Opinion Determinations of Crime*, 60 Duquesne Univ. Law Rev. 302 (2022) https://dsc.duq.edu/dlr/vol60/iss2/8/

Hanzlick, R., *Overview of the Medicolegal Death Investigation System in the United States* (2003). National Academies Press.

Kukucka, J. and Famulegun, O., *"Not Scientific" to Whom? Laypeople Misjudge Manner of Death Determinations as Scientific and Definitive*, 5 The Wrongful Conviction Law Review 1 (2024) https://wclawr.org/index.php/wclr/article/view/109

National Commission on Forensic Science, *Certification of Medicolegal Death Investigators* (2015) https://www.justice.gov/sites/default/files/ncfs/pages/attachments/2015/01/21/mdicertificationfinal.pdf

National Institute of Standards and Technology, *Medical Examiner* (2025) https://www.nist.gov/glossary-term/43651

National Research Council of the National Academies of Science, *Analysis of Hair Evidence, Strengthening Forensic Science in the United States: A Path Forward* (2009) https://nap.nationalacademies.org/catalog/12589/strengthening-forensic-science-in-the-united-states-a-path-forward

Sippio v. State, 350 Md. 633, 714 A.2d 864 (1998)

State v. Tyler, 867 N.W.2d 136 (Iowa 2015)

READINGS

American Board of Independent Medical Examiners, *Certified Independent Medical Examiner,* https://www.abime.org/wp-content/uploads/2019/12/CIME_Requreiments_Info_Sheet.pdf

International Association of Coroners and Medical Examiners, *Accreditation,* https://theiacme.com/page/accreditation

Medicolegal Death-Investigation Working Group, National Commission on Forensic Science, *View of the Commission, Certification of Medicolegal Death Investigators,* U.S. Department of Justice and National Institute of Standards and Technology (2015) https://www.justice.gov/ncfs/file/788026/download

Medicolegal-Death-Investigation Working Group, National Commission on Forensic Science, *Strengthening the Medico-Legal-Death-Investigation Accreditation and Certification a Path Forward,* National Science and Technology Council (2016) https://www.ojp.gov/pdffiles1/NIJ/251424.pdf

National Association of Medical Examiners, *Inspection and Accreditation,* https://www.thename.org/inspection-accreditation

National Institute of Justice, *The Daunting Task of Strengthening Medical Examiner and Coroner Investigations Across Hundreds of Jurisdictions,* U.S. Department of Justice, (April 24, 2024) https://nij.ojp.gov/topics/articles/daunting-task-strengthening-medical-examiner-and-coroner-investigations-across

Weedn, V., *Bases of Forensic Pathology Expert Testimony with Emphasis on Iowa v. Tyler,* 11 Acad. Forensic Pathol. 4 (2021) https://journals.sagepub.com/doi/abs/10.1177/19253621211060961

Part IV

The Use of Forensic Science out of Court

17

Non-Criminal and Administrative Investigations

So far, the focus has been on the admissibility of forensic science in the criminal case courtroom. The rules for allowing such testimony, as set forth in *Frye*, *Daubert*, and the rules of evidence, are understandably designed to make sure that only reliable scientific evidence is used in a proceeding that can deprive someone of their liberty or even their life. However, forensic science can also be valuable in other important but less life-altering situations. In civil or private matters or in administrative or regulatory processes, neither *Frye* nor *Daubert* or the rules of evidence necessarily apply. A few of those applications of forensic science outside of the courtroom are discussed in this chapter.

17.1 FORENSIC ODONTOLOGY (NOT BITE MARKS!)

Forensic odontology is the use of teeth and oral structures to make an identification. The use of bite marks in criminal prosecutions has been thoroughly discredited (Saurwein 2023) but forensic odontology is an important technique in the identification of the remains of victims in a mass disaster, attack, or other incidents where the identification of the human remains is not apparent. Disaster Victim Identification, or DVI, is the method used to identify victims of mass casualty incidents, either man-made or natural. Interpol, Disaster Victim Identification (DVI) (n.d.). DVI using odontology has been employed in terrorist attacks, transportation

DOI: 10.4324/9781041136361-21

accidents, fires, and earthquakes. "The forensic dentist is one of the key persons who plays an important role in the DVI human identification process." Pittayapat (2012).

Teeth are some of the hardest body structures, can withstand extreme heat, and are very slow to decompose after death. A forensic odontologist can compare the remaining tooth structures in a decedent with potential pre-death dental records to make an identification. Even if earlier dental records are not available, an odontologist may be able to determine the age, gender, and ethnicity, and perhaps the habits or occupations, of the decedent. That information can be important in making an eventual identification (Figure 17.1).

On September 11, 2001, terrorists hijacked four airliners. Two of them were crashed into the World Trade Center in New York City, one into the Pentagon in Washington, D.C., and the last crashed in a field in Pennsylvania. The attacks killed almost 3,000 people. At the World Trade Center, the crashes caused explosions and fires caused the giant buildings

Figure 17.1 911 World Trade Center Attack.

Source: Department of Defense

to collapse. The intense heat and the weight of the crumbling structures left many of the human victims unidentifiable. Over 200 dentists worked around the clock for almost a year to identify the victims. In the end, they were able to properly identify 1,000 of the 3,000 human remains (Davis, 2021).

17.2 DEATH CERTIFICATES

As we have discussed, medical examiners and other health care personnel are required by statutes to make a report of death indicating the cause and manner of death. These death certificates are important for many purposes other than criminal proceedings. A death certificate states the cause and manner of death, location and time of death, and other personal information about the decedent (Kircher, 1987).

For private matters, the death certificate serves as proof of the death. Most often, it is important for such things as life insurance, pension benefits, estate proceedings, and funeral arrangements. However, the certificate also serves as the basis for public health officials to compile important statistics about mortality data and contributing illnesses or injuries. The data are also important for compiling actuarial data concerning life expectancy. The National Death Index is an important database of death certificate information maintained by the Center for Disease Control.

17.3 POLYGRAPHS

The theory of a lie detector is that it can detect truthfulness or deception by monitoring psychophysiological changes in response to questioning. The machine measures respiration, cardiovascular activity (blood pressure), and skin conductivity. The federal law defines a lie detector as a "device (whether mechanical or electrical) that is used, or the results of which are used, for the purpose of rendering a diagnostic opinion regarding the honesty or dishonesty of an individual." A polygraph is "an instrument that . . . records changes in cardiovascular, respiratory, and electrodermal . . . and . . . is used . . . for the purpose of rendering a diagnostic opinion regarding the honesty or dishonesty of an individual."

Since the *Frye* case, American courts have consistently held that lie detectors, or polygraphs, are not reliable or admissible in criminal cases to prove truthfulness or deception. Most scientists and criminal courts believe there is no evidence that any pattern of physiological reactions is unique to deception. Nevertheless, polygraphs continue to be used outside of court for a variety of non-judicial reasons.

Federal law, and some State laws, prohibit employers from using lie detectors in hiring or firing employees. The federal Employee Polygraph Protection Act of 1988 makes it unlawful for any employer to require a potential or current employee to take a polygraph or to base any job action on the results of a polygraph. Employee Polygraph Protection Act of 1988 (EPPA), 29 USC §2001 et seq.

> Except as provided in sections 7 and 8, it shall be unlawful for any employer engaged in or affecting commerce or in the production of goods for commerce – (1) directly or indirectly, to require, request, suggest, or cause any employee or prospective employee to take or submit to any lie detector test.
>
> Employee Polygraph Protection Act of 1988

However, the law makes important exceptions. First, it specifically does not apply to "the United States Government, any State or local government, or any political subdivision of a State or local government." Therefore, unless a State law provides otherwise, prospective or current government employees can be required to take a lie detector test, and the government may use the results in making personnel decisions. It also allows the use of lie detectors for any intelligence or counter-intelligence purposes. Second, the federal law makes a broad specific exception for private employers to use a polygraph in connection with "an ongoing investigation involving economic loss or injury to the employer's business, such as theft, embezzlement, misappropriation, or an act of unlawful industrial espionage or sabotage." Employee Polygraph Protection Act of 1988 (EPPA), 29 USC §2001 et seq

REFERENCES

Davis, C., *Remembering 9/11: Local Dentist Remembers Effort to Identify the Victims*, NewsChannel5 (September 10, 2021) https://www.newschannel5.com/news/remembering-9-11-local-dentist-remembers-effort-to-identify-the-victims

Employee Polygraph Protection Act of 1988 (EPPA), 29 USC §2001 et seq

Interpol, Disaster Victim Identification (DVI) (n.d.) https://www.interpol.int/en/How-we-work/Forensics/Disaster-Victim-Identification-DVI

Kircher, T. and Anderson, R., *Cause of Death: Proper Completion of the Death Certificate*, 258(3) JAMA 349–352 (1987) https://doi.org/10.1001/jama.1987.03400030065033

National Center for Health Statisics, *National Death Index*, Center for Disease Control (2024) https://www.cdc.gov/nchs/ndi/index.html

Pittayapat, P., et al., *Forensic Odontology in the Disaster Victim Identification Process*, J. Forensic Odontostomatol. (2012) https://pmc.ncbi.nlm.nih.gov/articles/PMC5734849/

Sauerwein, K., et al., *Bitemark Analysis: A NIST Scientific Foundation Review*, National Institute of Standards & Technology (2023) https://nvlpubs.nist.gov/nistpubs/ir/2023/NIST.IR.8352.pdf

READINGS

MacDorman, M., et al., *Racial and Ethnic Disparities in Maternal Mortality in the United States Using Enhanced Vital Records, 2016–2017*, 111 Am. J. Pub. Health 1673 (2021) https://doi.org/10.2105/AJPH.2021.306375

Miller, R., *Forensic Odontology in Disaster Victim Identification*, 69 J. Forensic Sci. 1630–1636 (2024) https://doi.org/10.1111/1556-4029.15471

National Research Council, *The Polygraph and Lie Detection* (2003). The National Academies Press. https://doi.org/10.17226/10420

Stromberg, J., *Lie Detectors: Why They Don't Work, and Why Police Use Them Anyway*, Vox.com (2014) https://www.vox.com/2014/8/14/5999119/polygraphs-lie-detectors-do-they-work

18

Criminal Investigations (Narrowing the Field)

18.1 PATTERN IDENTIFICATIONS AND POLYGRAPHS

As we have discussed, there are several reliability concerns under *Daubert*, *Frye*, and the rules of evidence that affect the admissibility of several forms of pattern identification. While these analyses may not be sufficient proof of guilt in a criminal trial, they may nevertheless be valuable investigation tools for the police. They can help police exclude a group of potential suspects based on their characteristics or they may help police focus on another group of potential suspects that share an observable characteristic. Using fingerprints, footwear, microscopic hair analysis, or even bite marks can effectively exclude possible suspects and narrow the field for further investigation (Figure 18.1).

While polygraphs are not admissible evidence, many police agencies use them for investigative purposes (National Research Council, 2003). Police believe that the polygraph can be an effective tool to eliminate subjects. The lie detector has been used as an element of interrogation. A trained polygraph operator often uses the machine, or the threat of it, to convince a suspect to tell the truth and even confess. Some studies indicate that 25–50% of interrogated suspects confess to the crime, having become convinced that they have proven to be dishonest by the machine. (Desroches and Thomas, 1985).

DOI: 10.4324/9781041136361-22

Figure 18.1 Polygraph Examination.

Source: Lewis & Dickstein LLC

18.2 FACIAL RECOGNITION

Facial recognition software maps a person's facial features mathematically and then uses algorithms to compare the digital image to a database of stored face prints. The program identifies approximately 80 points on a human face using variables like nose length and width, eye socket depth, and cheekbone shape. If the subject's face is partially obscured or in profile the software is less reliable. One researcher characterized facial recognition technology as a "double-edged sword":

> In recent years, facial recognition technology (FRT) has emerged as a double-edged sword, offering significant benefits across various societal sectors while simultaneously presenting complex ethical, legal, and personal challenges. . . . This technology, which identifies and verifies individuals by analyzing facial features from videos or images, has become increasingly integrated into daily life and institutional governance. . . . Its applications range from enhancing security protocols and consumer experiences to streamlining administrative processes, marking a notable improvement in operational efficiency . . . However, the rapid adoption of FRT in these areas raises important questions about individual privacy, data security, and ethical implications, necessitating a thorough academic examination that goes beyond superficial benefits.
>
> Wang (2024)

Although facial recognition software is now common for authentication purposes, like Smartphones, Facebook, or other social media, it has also been used for law enforcement investigations to identify potential suspects. Recent laboratory testing of facial recognition software programs has shown that many of the programs are over 99% accurate (Lewis, 2021). However, that level of accuracy drops almost 10% in real life applications, particularly in law enforcement. In real life situations, lighting variations, non-frontal angles, masks, glasses, and other face coverings, and low-resolution images from surveillance cameras can all significantly reduce recognition accuracy (Figure 18.2).

There are significant concerns about the use of facial recognition software, especially by law enforcement. There is some evidence that facial recognition systems have higher error rates for people of color, especially women, as opposed to white males. Lohr (2022) This bias can lead to misidentification, wrongful arrests, and increased surveillance in marginalized communities. Some studies also indicate biases based on

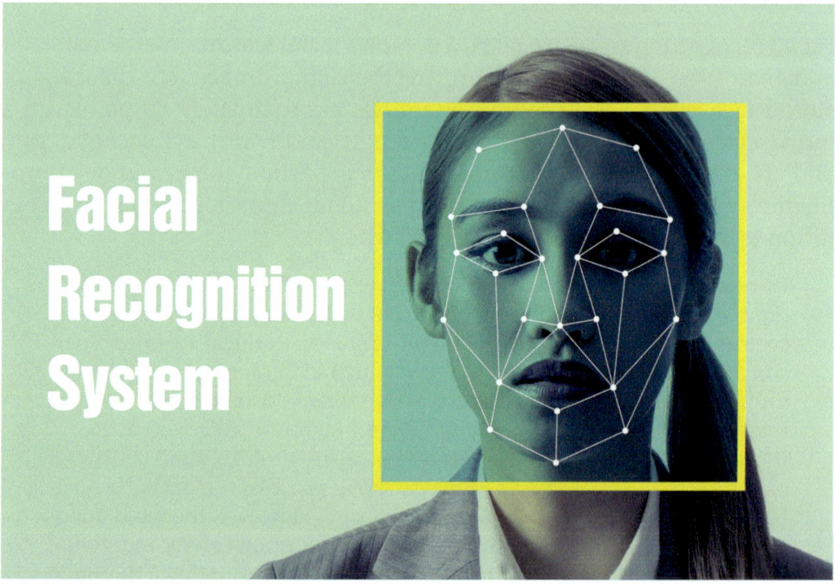

Figure 18.2 Facial Recognition Software.

Source: metamorworks

age and gender. The National Institute of Standards and Technology has conducted evaluations of various facial recognition software programs as to the performance and accuracy of facial recognition algorithms and vendors (National Institute of Standards and Technology, 2025).

18.3 GENETIC GENEALOGY

Law enforcement professionals and genealogy professionals have pioneered a new way of using DNA genealogical databases to solve crimes. Beginning with the publication of the arrest of a man in the decades-old case of the "Golden State Killer," police across the country have been utilizing DNA-based genealogical databases to develop family trees from crime scene DNA, isolate relatives, and then use common genealogical techniques to identify possible sources of the crime scene DNA (Bieber, 2006). It has led to arrests in dozens of previously cold cases.

Genealogy is the retrieval of family information data from various private and public records and putting it into meaningful relationship patterns. It is the discovery of data like names, dates, places of birth, marriages, and deaths and also includes occupations, migration data, and other information found in censuses and wills and other estate documents. The data allows an experienced genealogist to organize a "family tree" by pedigree working backward or by lineage working forward from an ancestor to descendants. The internet greatly expanded the ability of genealogists to trace lineage, but the advent of DNA was the real revolution in genealogy. Understanding and mapping the human genome made it possible to trace the ancestry of humans with the utmost accuracy. The family tree was now occupied by direct branches of genes instead of circumstantial evidence based on human recollection and records.

As discussed earlier, the government maintains a DNA database called CODIS. When police submit a profile of a DNA sample they have collected at a crime scene, such as from a rape kit or blood, a search of CODIS may reveal a potential match to a suspect. But there are limitations in CODIS. Most importantly, there will only be a match if that suspect has a prior conviction or arrest that resulted in a government DNA profile. Second, the type of genetic information stored in CODIS is limited and not very useful in finding potential relatives. The use of genetic genealogy assumes that the police have been unable to find a corresponding sample in CODIS.

Several years ago, commercial genealogy sites, like Ancestry.com and 23andMe, started offering sophisticated DNA testing to the general public over the Internet. Using existing databases and DNA samples submitted by its customers, a consumer could obtain geographic and national origin information about their ancestry. The companies also provided a means by which the consumer can send a message to other submitters who may be relatives based on the data, but the other submitters are usually not identified by name, location, or otherwise. It is estimated that over 100 million people have used these direct-to-consumer websites (Shelton, 2020).

The raw data from DNA analysis contains much more genetic information than is reflected in the generalized geographic reports. The major commercial genealogy sites provide customers with the option of downloading their raw genetic data, more recently in terms of SNPs containing much more genetic information than is stored in CODIS.

Enter GEDmatch. GEDmatch was a database and website developed by two Florida men as a free tool to help people identify their relatives by comparing their raw DNA data to other interested people who also decided to submit their raw data to the GEDmatch database. It grew very quickly in popularity. What was special about GEDmatch was that it identified additional unknown cousins who did not test at the same commercial company, it could determine specifically the amount of DNA shared with others, and it provided additional matches that were not identified by the consumer testing company due to the algorithms they used. Importantly, the GEDmatch results provided the email address of the matching cousins, thus making them identifiable. GEDmatch has subsequently been sold to much larger companies but it is still available to the public – and to the police (GEDmatch, n.d.).

Combining genetic genealogy and traditional genealogy is the essence of genetic genealogy crime solving. Genetic genealogy provides direct scientific evidence of the ancestral relationship between the person who left the evidence at the crime scene and several potential relatives. Traditional genealogy then uses classic genealogical records data to provide circumstantial evidence of the probable specific relative, based primarily on demographic and geographic characteristics of the crime. So, the police analyze, either themselves or through a commercial source, the DNA from a crime scene. They then submit the raw data from that crime scene DNA to a GEDmatch company. If they find a common ancestor, an experienced genealogist can then construct a family tree working down from that ancestor and possibly find several contemporaneous cousins to the suspect. Then the real detective work starts. Using public sources, they can investigate which of those might be the suspect based on location, age, gender, physical characteristics, and other factors (Greytak, 2019; Glynn, 2022).

For many reasons, especially the hearsay basis of much traditional genealogy information, the results of a genetic genealogy search would not be admissible in a criminal trial. Instead, the police treat the information as a tip or lead for further investigation. Typically, police will get DNA from the identified suspect from discarded objects that have DNA from the suspect. They will then get a direct laboratory comparison of that sample to the crime scene, and that will give them probable cause to get a warrant to take a current sample of DNA to further compare the samples.

Several privacy and 4th Amendment concerns have been raised concerning genetic genealogy. The defendant clearly has no valid objection to the examination of DNA from something he left at the crime scene. A basic principle of constitutional law is that there is no reasonable expectation of privacy in property which has been abandoned. Abel v. United States, 362 U.S. 217, 241 (1960). Similarly, when the police subsequently get a sample of DNA from an object that the identified suspect has discarded, the principle of abandonment precludes any 4th Amendment objection. There is no expectation of privacy in garbage. California v. Greenwood, 86 U.S. 35 (1988) Nevertheless, a few States have adopted laws restricting but not prohibiting police use of abandoned DNA.

There have also been objections that the person who originally submitted their sample to the ancestry company did not understand that it might be used to implicate a distant relative in a crime. However, the defendant does not have any standing to complain that someone else's rights may have been violated. Rakas v. Illinois, 439 U.S. 128 (1978)

The commercial companies have implemented measures designed to ensure that their customers give their informed consent to such use of their sample for possible police examination. It has recently been held that even if those private rules were violated, the defendant has no standing to object to the use of that information. In the recent case of a man charged with the murder of four college students in Idaho, the judge addressed such a claim, stating "With regard to the violation of the databases' user policies, while this may give rise to civil action between the FBI and the particular database or perhaps the individuals whose DNA profiles were used, Defendant has not explained how this implicates the Fourth Amendment." State v. Kohberger (February 17, 2025). A few States have adopted laws restricting but not prohibiting police use of genetic genealogy in criminal investigations. Montana Code § 44-6-104 (2021); Massachusetts General Laws, MGL - Part I, Title XVI, Chapter 111, Section 70G (2025); Utah Code 53-10-403.7 (2024).

CASE STUDY The Golden State Killer

Beginning in 1974, an individual in California began committing a series of burglaries, rapes, and murders. Over the next 12 years, he perpetrated at least 51 rapes, including one 15-year-old victim. Often, he would stalk women who were alone in their homes but later began attacking couples, binding the male and repeatedly raping the female. He initially murdered three people between 1974 and 1979. From 1979 to 1986, he murdered ten more people in several California locations. He shot all his murder victims. During his active period, he committed over 140 burglaries of homes. In 1986, the crimes stopped.

Although police eventually realized that the crimes were probably the result of one perpetrator, several leads produced no results. Police had several crime scene DNA samples, but CODIS did not find any match. All of the crimes went unsolved for the next 30 years.

In 2016, the FBI released information about the killer, who had become known as the "Golden State Killer," and a $50,000 reward was offered. In 2017, an inspector from Contra Costa County had been working on the case for decades, heard about the idea of genetic genealogy and contacted Barabara Rae-Venter, a biologist, and for help. Rae-Venter uploaded a profile of the crime scene DNA to GEDmatch. It produced matches to several distant relatives she was able to build a family tree based on traditional genealogy research methods. She was able to work back to find a common ancestor, the great-great-great grandparents, and then work forward to identify the descendants. The investigators then eliminated individuals who were not suspects based on age, ethnicity, location, and other factors. From 20 possible suspects, they narrowed it to two, and one of those was eliminated based on a DNA sample. The remaining suspect was identified as Joeseph DeAngelo, who had actually been a California police officer during the early crimes (Figure 18.3).

After the identification, investigators collected DNA samples from the door handle of DeAngelo's car, and from a tissue found in his garbage can. Both were matched to samples associated with

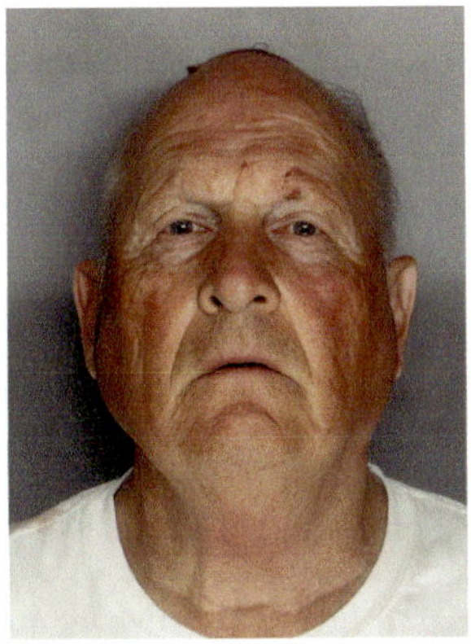

Figure 18.3 Joseph DeAngelo Mug Shot.

the Golden State Killer crimes. Those samples were then compared directly to the crime scene samples and DeAngelo was arrested on April 24, 2018.

On June 29, 2020, as part of a plea bargain removing the death penalty, DeAngelo pled guilty to 13 counts of first-degree murder and 13 counts of kidnapping. He was sentenced to multiple life sentences without the possibility of parole.

REFERENCES

Abel v. United States, 362 U.S. 217, 241(1960)

Bieber, F., et al., *Human Genetics. Finding Criminals through DNA of Their Relatives*, 312(5778) Science 1315–1316 (2006) https://pubmed.ncbi.nlm.nih.gov/16690817/

California v. Greenwood, 86 U.S. 35 (1988)

Desroches, F. and Thomas, A., *The Police Use of the Polygraph in Criminal Investigations*, 27 Canadian J. Crim. 1 (January, 1985) https://utppublishing.com/doi/10.3138/cjcrim.27.1.43

GEDmatch, *Where DNA Connections Come Together* (n.d.) https://www.gedmatch.com/

Glynn, C., *Bridging Disciplines to Form a New One: The Emergence of Forensic Genetic Genealogy*, 1 Genes (Basel) 13 (2022) https://www.mdpi.com/2073-4425/13/8/1381

Greytak, E., Moore, C. and Armentrout, S., *Genetic Genealogy for Cold Case and Active Investigations*, 299 Forensic Sci. Int. 103 (2019) https://www.sciencedirect.com/science/article/abs/pii/S0379073819301264?via%3Dihub

Lewis, J. and Crumpler, W., *How Does Facial Recognition Work?* Center for Strategic & International Studies (June 10, 2021) https://www.csis.org/analysis/how-does-facial-recognition-work

Lohr, S., *Facial Recognition is Accurate, If You're a White Guy**, chapter in *Ethics of Data and Analytics* (2022). Auerbach Publications. https://www.taylorfrancis.com/chapters/edit/10.1201/9781003278290-22/facial-recognition-accurate-re-white-guy-steve-lohr

Massachusetts General Laws, MGL - Part I, Title XVI, Chapter 111, Section 70G (2025) https://malegislature.gov/Laws/GeneralLaws/PartI/TitleXVI/Chapter111/Section70G

Montana Code § 44-6-104 (2021) https://archive.legmt.gov/bills/mca/title_0440/chapter_0060/part_0010/section_0040/0440-0060-0010-0040.html

National Institute of Standards and technology, *Face Recognition Vendor Test (FRVT)* (2025) https://www.nist.gov/programs-projects/face-recognition-vendor-test-frvt

National Research Council, *The Polygraph and Lie Detection* (2003). The National Academies Press. https://nap.nationalacademies.org/catalog/10420/the-polygraph-and-lie-detection

Shelton, D., *Genetic Genealogy and Law Enforcement: New Bedfellows SSRN* (February 21, 2020) http:/dx.doi.org/10.2139/ssrn.5153995

State v. Kohberger, *Order on Defendant's Motion to Suppress re: Genetic Information* (February 17, 2025) https://coi.isc.idaho.gov/docs/CR01-24-31665/2025/021925-Order-Defendants-Motion-Suppress-Genetic-Information.pdf

Utah Code 53-10-403.7 (2024) https://le.utah.gov/xcode/Title53/Chapter10/53-10-S403.7.html?v=C53-10-S403.7_2023050320230503#:~:text=Before%20an%20individual%20may%20be,(iii)

Wang, X., et al., *Beyond Surveillance: Privacy, Ethics, and Regulations in Face Recognition Technology*, Front. Big Data (2024) https://pmc.ncbi.nlm.nih.gov/articles/PMC11256005/

READINGS

Akpan, N., *Genetic Genealogy Can Help Solve Cold Cases: It Can Also Accuse the Wrong Person*, PBS News (November 7, 2019) https://www.pbs.org/newshour/science/genetic-genealogy-can-help-solve-cold-cases-it-can-also-accuse-the-wrong-person

Berkman, B., Miller, W. and Grady, C., *Is It Ethical to Use Genealogy Data to Solve Crimes?* 4 Ann. Intern. Med. 169 (2018) https://www.acpjournals.org/doi/10.7326/M18-1348

Bryan, K., *Lawmakers Cautious as Genetic Tests Help in Cracking Cold Cases*, National Conference of State Legislatures (October 23, 2023) https://www.ncsl.org/state-legislatures-news/details/lawmakers-cautious-as-genetic-tests-help-in-cracking-cold-cases

Cavallier, A., *How 'Trash' is Helping Police Catch Murder Suspects Decades Later*, Independent (July 1, 2024) https://www.the-independent.com/news/world/americas/crime/trash-solves-cold-cases-murder-suspects-b2572125.html

Global Polygraph Network, *Why Are Polygraph Tests Used in Criminal Investigations?* (March 26, 2025) https://www.polytest.org/why-are-polygraph-tests-used-in-criminal-investigations/

Golda, A., et al., *Privacy and Security Concerns in Generative AI: A Comprehensive Survey*, 12 IEEE Access 48126 (2024) https://ieeexplore.ieee.org/abstract/document/10478883

Jiminez, K., *Discarded DNA: The Controversial Clue in the Trash That's Bringing Serial Killers to Justice*, USA Today (July 21, 2013) https://www.usatoday.com/story/news/nation/2023/07/20/police-are-using-surreptitious-dna-collection-to-solve-cold-murder-cases/70427941007/

Kim, J., *The FBI and Other Agencies Are using Polygraphs to Find Leakers: But do They Work?* NPR (April 30, 2025) https://www.npr.org/2025/04/30/g-s1-63349/fbi-polygraph-lie-detector-leak-investigation

Moore, C., *CeCe Moore Explains How Genetic Genealogy Works*, YouTube, https://www.youtube.com/watch?v=8Jr_xAJRh9U

Paravision, Introduction to NIST FRVT (2023) https://www.paravision.ai/news/introduction-to-nist-frvt/

Shelton, D. and Bieber, F., *The Theory of Criminal Relativity: Using Genealogy Databases to Solve Crimes*, SSRN (February 21, 2019) https://papers.ssrn.com/sol3/papers.cfm?abstract_id=5153990

Smith, M. and Miller, S., *The Ethical Application of Biometric Facial Recognition Technology*, 37 AI & Society 167 (2022) https://link.springer.com/article/10.1007/S00146-021-01199-9

Tuazon, O., et al., *Law Enforcement Use of Genetic Genealogy Databases in Criminal Investigations: Nomenclature, Definition and Scope*, 8 Forensic Sci. Int. Synerg. 8 (2024) https://www.sciencedirect.com/science/article/pii/S2589871X2400007X?via%3Dihub

Wickenheiser, R., *Forensic Genealogy, Bioethics and the Golden State Killer Case*, 12 Forensic Sci. Int. Synerg. 114 (2019) https://www.sciencedirect.com/science/article/pii/S2589871X19301342?via%3Dihub

Part V

The Future of Forensic Science Evidence

19

Artificial Intelligence

19.1 FORENSIC SCIENCE APPLICATIONS OF ARTIFICIAL INTELLIGENCE

AI is the use of computer systems and machines to perform tasks that normally require human intelligence. Generative AI means that the machine generates new content based on patterns in data it is fed and the algorithms built into the computer. Generative AI is revolutionizing communication, work, and innovation in many fields (National Institute of Standards and Technology, 2025). AI programs have been used in some forensic science applications for several years. They have been used in crime scene reconstruction, forensic imaging, voice analysis, and other criminal justice situations. AI has been part of the rapid advancement of DNA profiling techniques. In digital forensics, AI can be very useful in cybersecurity applications. Nevertheless, the majority of forensic science laboratories have yet to adopt many AI systems.

The use of generative AI in forensic science poses real opportunities. Generative AI offers many potential benefits, enabling users to automate, augment, and accelerate a wide range of workflows. One of the most promising aspects of AI is its ability to process, search, classify, and even interpret the massive amounts of data that are often involved in forensic science applications. For example, AI technology can improve the speed of fingerprint analysis by automating fingerprint comparison, enhancing latent prints and identifying unique features. There are similar advantages in ballistics and other pattern identification disciplines. AI technology may reduce the risk of human error. Johns Hopkins Univ. (2025)

DOI: 10.4324/9781041136361-24

19.2 THE ADMISSIBILITY OF AI-GENERATED EVIDENCE

Recently, the Supreme Court adopted several key amendments to the Federal Rules, including the creation of a new provision: Federal Rule of Evidence 707. The Comment to the Rule says "This newly adopted rule is designed to address growing concerns around the use of AI-generated evidence, particularly when such evidence functions similarly to expert testimony and raises parallel questions of reliability, bias, error, and interpretability." Fed. R. Evid. 707

RULE 707 MACHINE-GENERATED EVIDENCE

When machine-generated evidence is offered without an expert witness and would be subject to Rule 702 if testified to by a witness, the court may admit the evidence only it if satisfies the requirements of Rule 702 (a)-(d). This rule does not apply to the output of basic scientific instruments. (emphasis added)

Remember that Rule 702 (a)–(d) requires the following:

(a) The expert's scientific, technical, or other specialized knowledge will help the trier of fact to understand the evidence or to determine a fact in issue.
(b) The testimony is based on sufficient facts or data.
(c) The testimony is the product of reliable principles and methods.
(d) The expert has reliably applied expert's opinion reflects a reliable application of the principles and methods to the facts of the case.

This means that AI-generated evidence, standing alone, must meet the reliability requirements of *Daubert* and be reliably applied to the case at hand.

In the current state of AI-generated forensic science evidence, that will be difficult. Most programs have not been tested to the point where there is a demonstrable error rate. There are no industry or professional standards for such programs, and each program depends on the algorithms built into it. Peer review requires review by forensic scientists in the particular field and that has not yet been forthcoming. Likewise, there is no indication yet that such evidence has been generally accepted in any specific forensic-science discipline. All of those factors may change in the future, but it will take some time.

19.3 LEGAL SYSTEM REACTIONS TO AI

AI-generated evidence may also have difficulty getting past the judicial gatekeepers for other reasons. Lawyers quickly welcomed AI with open arms and have tried to use it liberally in their law practice and in court. They have found that AI can be especially useful in doing legal research and even generating briefs to support their position in court. It can replace expensive hours of research by associates. It can therefore have an equalizing effect between large law firms and small or solo practitioners (Figure 19.1).

The embracement of AI is not shared by the judiciary. For a lot of reasons, many judges regard AI with an attitude somewhere between fear and loathing. This is new stuff and, as discussed in the chapter on science and the law, judges prefer the status quo don't do "new". And

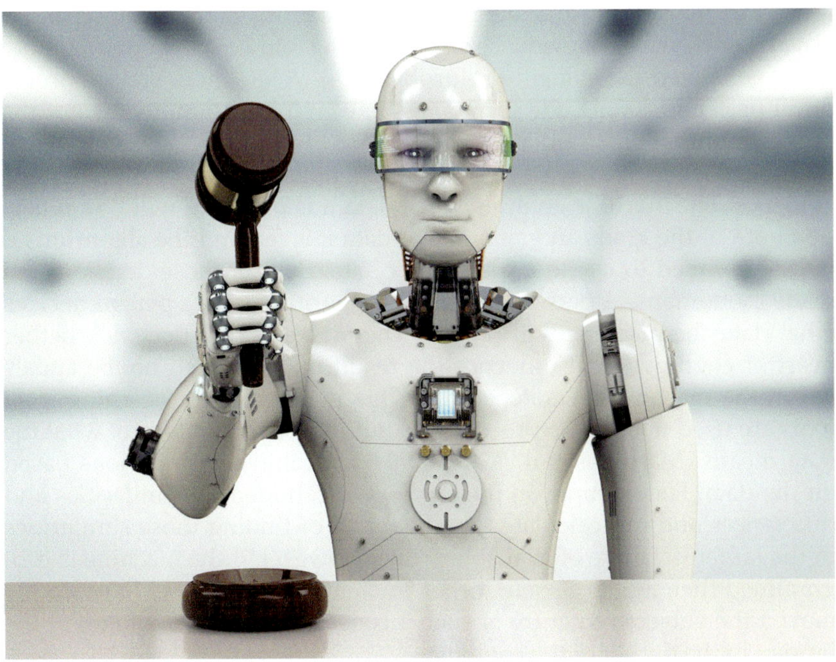

Figure 19.1 Judges and AI.

Source: iStock

the initial experience of many judges with AI has raised serious questions about its authenticity and reliability. The AI-generated legal briefs contained fictitious cases that the program generated to bolster the position that the lawyer espoused. One study found that ChatGPT fabricated, or "hallucinated", between 15% and 55% of its case citations (Charlotin, n.d.). Judges have found attorneys in contempt and imposed sanctions for using such programs (Bellas, 2025).

19.4 CONCERNS ABOUT AI AND JUSTICE

AI programs pose significant issues regarding the discovery of how their information is generated. Most AI programs have been commercially developed, and their owners regard the source code for the algorithms in those programs as trade secrets. However, the defendant has a constitutional right to confront the witnesses and to cross-examine them. Moreover, the judge cannot determine the reliability of the machine under *Daubert* or the rules of evidence without being told how it works and how it has generated the evidence (Murphy, 2024). While there may be procedural protections for trade secrets in some civil litigation, that is not the case in criminal prosecutions.

There is a legitimate concern about the potential bias of AI-generated evidence. The machine analysis of the data it is provided will be a reflection both of the kinds and amounts of data it is fed and the algorithms it is programmed to use to evaluate that data. Both of those decisions are made by humans. A person designs the algorithm, and a person decides what data the machine will receive. The biases of that person, whether overt or cognitive, will influence the result but may well not be apparent in the machine-generated result. This is especially concerning if AI tools are used not only to process data but then also to interpret what the data means. Machines can clearly make probabilistic projections based on the data. For example, in fingerprints, it can identify similarities and differences and can calculate the likelihood of finding those similarities in the larger database of available prints. However, if the machine is programmed then to make some sort of "match" conclusion, we have simply moved the subjective nature of such a conclusion from the mouth of the human to the output of the computer.

There is a potential problem that jurors may overvalue the importance of machine-generated evidence. The problem is the potential for "blind acceptance" of computer results. Our society has undergone such rapid and overwhelming advancements in information technology that it is easy to assume that the information we get from our computers, or our "smartphones" is accurate. Studies have shown that jurors expect and demand scientific evidence in criminal trials and presenting evidence from an intelligent machine can play into that expectation and demand.

There is also a concern that the use of AI and other advanced technologies may exacerbate the inequalities in our criminal justice system. The government has all of the technological tools at its disposal, but the defendant and defense counsel usually have no such resources. We already see this in the availability of expert witnesses generally, where the prosecution can use forensic science experts who are already paid employees of the government or can go out and hire experts to testify. The defense has no in-house forensic science experts, little or no expertise in even knowing what kind of expert is needed, and has to ask the judge for some money to find an expert. Neither the public defender office nor the office of an appointed defense attorney will typically even have a subscription to an AI program.

REFERENCES

Bellas, G., *Deepfakes in the Courtroom: Problems and Solutions*, 55 Bench & Bar 5, Illinois State Bar Association (March 2025) https://www.isba.org/sections/bench/newsletter/2025/03/deepfakesinthecourtroomproblemsandsolutions

Charlotin, D., *AI Hallucinations* (n.d.) https://www.damiencharlotin.com/hallucinations/

Fed. R. Evid. 702

Fed. R. Evid. 707

Johns Hopkins University, *The Future of Forensics – How AI Can Transform Investigations* (August 26, 2025) https://washingtondc.jhu.edu/news/ai-in-forensics/

Murphy, N., *Give Me Liberty or Give Me the Source Code: Challenging a BlackBox Computer Algorithm Under Daubert*, 30 Richmond J. Law Tech. 2 (2024) https://scholarship.richmond.edu/jolt/vol30/iss2/2/?

National Institute of Standards and Technology and RTI International, *Harnessing AI for Forensics Symposium, Keynote Panel*, Washington, DC (July 9, 2025) https://youtu.be/nG5pJwv8F-I?si=nR73hJz4tb7rIUAx

READINGS

Cwik, C., et al., *Artificial Intelligence, Trustworthiness, and Litigation. Artificial Intelligence and the Courts: Materials for Judges*, American Association for the Advancement of Science (2022) https://doi.org/10.1126/aaas.adf0786

Gaona, J., *The Role of AI in Forensics*, Marymount College (September 19, 2024) https://marymount.edu/blog/the-role-of-ai-in-forensics/

Gesser, A., et al., *Federal Judicial Conference to Revise Rules of Evidence to Address AI Risks*, Program on Corporate Compliance, KYU School of Law (March 7, 2025) https://wp.nyu.edu/compliance_enforcement/2025/03/27/federal-judicial-conference-to-revise-rules-of-evidence-to-address-ai-risks/

Langham, P., *Applying Daubert and Frye to AI Evidence*, Maryland State Bar Association (October 23, 2024) https://www.msba.org/site/site/content/News-and-Publications/News/General-News/Applying_Daubert_and_Frye_to_AI_Evidence.aspx

Maddox, I., *Artificial Intelligence in the Courtroom: Forensic Machines, Expert Witnesses, and the Confrontation Clause*, 15 Case W. Res. J. L. Tech. Internet 416 (2024) https://scholarlycommons.law.case.edu/jolti/vol15/iss2/6

20

Pathways to Improvement

20.1 IMPROVING FORENSIC SCIENCE EVIDENCE IN AN ADVERSARIAL JUSTICE SYSTEM

Despite the problems with forensic science evidence discovered by DNA and in wrongful convictions, the reality is that most criminal judges still routinely admit almost any expert testimony offered by prosecutors. Although the use of forensic science by prosecutors has increased dramatically, partially in response to the expectations and demands of jurors, the exclusion of such prosecution evidence by judges is relatively rare. Surveys indicate that *Daubert* challenges and hearings rarely occur.

In our adversarial justice system, judges usually can only exclude prosecution evidence if the defense attorney makes an objection to the admission of that evidence or at least requests a separate *Daubert* or *Frye* hearing regarding its admissibility. Even when objections are made, many judges do not either understand their gatekeeping responsibilities or have any knowledge about the inherent problems with some forms of forensic science disciplines. The NAS Report explained, "Lawyers and judges often have insufficient training and background in scientific methods, and they often fail to fully comprehend the approaches employed by different forensic science disciplines and the strengths and vulnerabilities of forensics science evidence offered during trials." It went further, "[t]he judicial system is encumbered by, among other things, judges and lawyers who generally lack the scientific expertise necessary to comprehend and evaluate forensic evidence in an informed manner." National Research Council (2009) at pp. 109–110.

DOI: 10.4324/9781041136361-25

The problem with defense lawyers and judges lack of understanding about forensic science evidence begins in law school. Again, the NAS Report recommended, "Law schools should enhance this connection by offering courses in the forensic science disciplines, by offering credit for forensic science courses taken in other colleges, and by developing joint degree programs." Nevertheless, with a few notable exceptions, law schools do not have programs with a curriculum that includes the fundamentals of forensic science evidence. Usually, it is only tangentially covered as a short subject about expert witness testimony in a much larger class on evidence. And in the few law school courses that are offered they are usually introductory classes with no information on statistics or scientific methods. The result is lawyers (who later become judges) with little or no understanding of scientific evidence or of their role in challenging such evidence. Law schools can change that if they choose to do so.

In our adversarial system, the onus for challenging forensic science is clearly on the defense attorney, who needs to learn about the forensic disciplines to prepare a defense. Many defense lawyers may not be familiar with the significant reliability problems of several traditional forms of forensic science evidence. To even understand when to file an objection or motion, the defense attorney needs to know which disciplines are subject to challenge, and why they may be. Some blame the lack of defense challenges on inadequately funded and overworked public defenders and appointed defense lawyers. Adequate funding and lowered caseloads are a partial answer to equipping defense attorneys to be competent in dealing with forensic science evidence.

After law school, most States require some form of continuing education for attorneys and, in some States, for judges as well. However, most of the continuing lawyer education programs focus on civil matters rather than criminal law, and the ones that deal with criminal law very rarely address forensic science issues. Further, most continuing education courses are commercial and funding for such attendance by public defenders is not often forthcoming. Appointed criminal defense lawyers usually have no source for funding continuing education courses other than their own funds, and the compensation for such appointments is minimal. A few States have publicly funded continuing education for public defenders but again, the offerings for forensic science evidence are slim or non-existent. Given the increasing reliance by prosecutors on forensic science evidence, continuing education for defense attorneys needs to be increased and even made mandatory.

The challenge to get judges to conduct meaningful hearings on the admissibility of forensic science evidence is difficult. The demonstrated resistance to excluding prosecution evidence may be the result of cognitive bias by judges who are often former prosecutors and who may be responding to a "tough on crime" electorate. Some continuing education programs are available for judges, and most States have some form of mandatory judicial continuing education. However, little of the content of these programs is addressed to forensic science (Frazier, 2023). In many States judges can complete their mandatory education requirements by such things as attending annual judge meetings. There have been some new forensic science training programs for judges by various organizations but again funding for attendance at such programs depends on local or State appropriations, which are often difficult to obtain. When judges have a substantial criminal case docket, continuing education about forensic science evidence and judicial gatekeeping responsibilities should be mandatory.

20.2 STATUTORY AND REGULATORY REFORM

The 2009 NAS Report was the result of a Congressional directive and resulted in a series of recommendations for legislative action to improve forensic science and the evidence it generates. The recommendations called for the creation of a federal organization that would mandate the research and testing to validate or discredit many traditional forms of forensic evidence. Prosecutors opposed all of these proposals, as did some federal departments and some expert witness organizations. Congress never enacted any of the recommendations. After legislative inaction, the executive branch attempted to take some measures to improve forensic science evidence.

In 2013, an executive order created the National Commission on Forensic Science (NCFS) to advise the Justice Department on forensic science issues. The NCFS included a variety of forensic science and criminal justice professionals and made several recommendations for forensic science evidence improvement. However, in 2017, the Attorney General appointed by President Trump abolished the commission (National Commission on Forensic Science, n.d.).

In 2010, President Obama rechartered the President's Council of Advisors on Science and Technology (PCAST) to "make policy recommendations in areas such as understanding of science, technology, and innovation." In 2015, President Obama asked the Council to recommend additional steps that could help ensure the validity of forensic evidence.

In response PCAST issued a report in 2016 that concluded that many traditional forensic science methods lacked sufficient scientific foundation and recommended further research to establish their reliability. PCAST also recommended that the Department of Justice not use evidence from some disciplines and that federal judges do not admit such evidence (President's Council of Advisors on Science and Technology, 2016). However, the Justice Department later rejected the PCAST findings and recommendations and stated that it would not follow them (Press Release, 2021).

Federal legislative action to improve forensic science evidence is unlikely. A few States, however, have sought to establish commissions and other structures that may improve the system (Figure 20.1). As of 2022, 21 States had some sort of forensic science oversight structure, including Massachusetts, Illinois, Montana, Missouri, Nebraska, North Carolina, and Texas, which have established forensic science commissions with varying responsibilities and powers (National Institute of Justice, 2022; National Association of Forensic Science Boards, 2025).

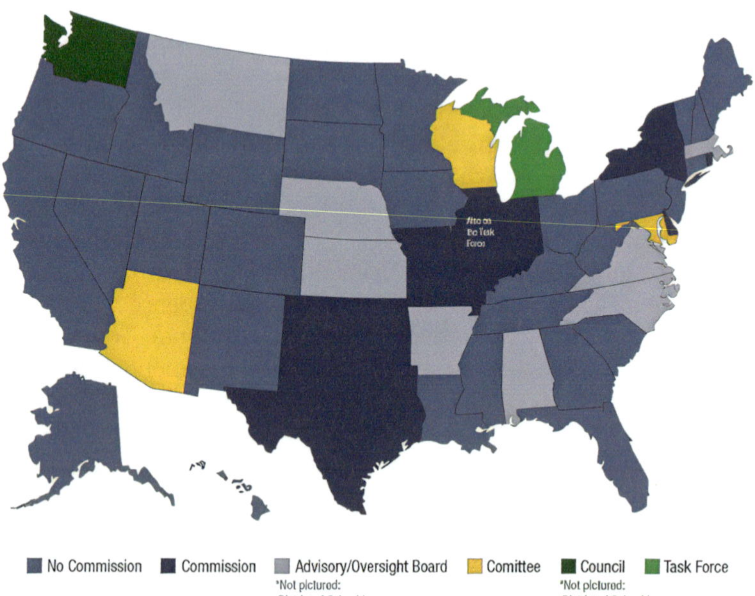

Figure 20.1 Forensic Science Oversight Organizations.

Source: National Institute of Justice

The Texas Forensic Science Commission is the most comprehensive and most active organization. It has the statutory power to undertake investigations for education and to; investigate allegations of professional negligence or misconduct (Texas Judicial Branch, 2025).

REFERENCES

Frazier, K., *An "F" in Judicial Education: Why Emerging Technologies and New Risks Demand Judicial Education Reform*, 50 Ohio N. Univ. L. Rev. (2023) https://digitalcommons.onu.edu/onu_law_review/vol50/iss1/2

National Association of Forensic Science Boards (2025) https://www.nafsb.org/

National Commission on Forensic Science, U.S. Department of Justice (n.d.) https://www.justice.gov/archives/ncfs

National Institute of Justice, *Forensic Science State Commissions and Oversight Bodies – 2022 Update*, U.S. Department of Justice (2022) https://www.ojp.gov/library/publications/forensic-science-state-commissions-and-oversight-bodies-2022-update

National Research Council of the National Academies of Science, *Analysis of Hair Evidence, Strengthening Forensic Science in the United States: A Path Forward* (2009) https://nap.nationalacademies.org/catalog/12589/strengthening-forensic-science-in-the-united-states-a-path-forward

President's Council of Advisors on Science and Technology (PCAST), *Report to the President, Forensic Science in Criminal Courts: Ensuring Scientific Validity of Feature-Comparison Method* (September, 2016) https://obamawhitehouse.archives.gov/sites/default/files/microsites/ostp/PCAST/pcast_forensic_science_report_final.pdf

Press Release, *Justice Department Publishes Statement on 2016 President's Council of Advisors on Science and Technology Report*, U.S. Department of Justice (January 13, 2021) https://www.justice.gov/archives/opa/pr/justice-department-publishes-statement-2016-presidents-council-advisors-science-and

Texas Judicial Branch, *Texas Forensic Science Commission* (2025) https://www.txcourts.gov/fsc/

READINGS

Forensic Science Reform: Protecting the Innocent, Koen, W. and Bowers, C. (Eds.) (2017). Academic Press.

Koehler, J., *Forensic Science Reform in the 21st Century: A Major Conference, a Blockbuster Report and Reasons to Be Pessimistic*, 9(1) Law, Probability & Risk, SSRN (2010) https://ssrn.com/abstract=1575957 or http://dx.doi.org/10.1093/lpr/mgp029

Shniderman, A., *Prosecutors Respond to Calls for Forensic Science Reform: More Sharks in Dirty Water*, 126 Yale L. J. F. 348 (2016) http://www.yalelawjournal.org/forum/prosecutors-respond-to-calls-for-forensic-science-reform

INDEX

Note: Page numbers in **bold** indicate a table and in *italics* indicate a figure.

B

C

D

J

K

L

M

N

O

P

Q

R

For Product Safety Concerns and Information please contact our EU representative GPSR@taylorandfrancis.com Taylor & Francis Verlag GmbH, Kaufingerstraße 24, 80331 München, Germany